CW00448730

PRAISE FOR

JESUS UNBOUND

"In his latest book, *Jesus Unbound*, Keith Giles continues to launch brilliant and practical theological flares for all those looking to stay centered on the path of a coherent Christianity. The preeminence of Christ applies to all things, even to Scriptures... *especially* to Scriptures. Obtaining the 'single eye' which Jesus said would 'fill our whole body with light' requires making the nature and Spirit of Christ our sole Rosetta Stone for understanding all Scriptural realties. Keith uses a witty, folksy, and irresistible style to show us that all the Scriptures must bend their interpretive knee to Jesus, not vice versa."

— RICHARD MURRAY, AUTHOR OF *THE JESUS MOOD*

"For those willing to step outside the theological box called 'biblical inerrancy,' this book is a goldmine. For those not willing, they're totally missing out. In *Jesus Unbound*, Keith Giles does the body of Christ a great service. Not only does he provide his readers with a lot to chew on, but he argues his points convincingly, yet gently and with pastoral care. An enjoyable read indeed!"

— MATTHEW J. DISTEFANO, AUTHOR OF 4 BOOKS AND CO-HOST OF THE *HERETIC HAPPY HOUR* PODCAST

"'The Word of God is living and active, sharper than any double-edged sword'...and when he was about 18, he grew a beard. Keith Giles runs with that company of Christ-followers committed to proclaiming that Jesus Christ is the Word of God, our final Authority for faith and practice. He most honors the Bible by refusing to confuse or conflate it with the Word-made-flesh. He hears the voice of Christ saying, 'These Scriptures testify of *me*.' The Lord warned that we can search the Scriptures diligently, yet never once hear the voice of his Father. How so? By becoming like confused puppies who stare at the tip of a pointing finger rather than gazing on the One to whom it is directed. Fear not: Keith does not throw the Bible under the bus. But he will dethrone biblical literalism wherever it supplants the Lordship of the whiskered Word of God."

— BRAD JERSAK, PHD, AUTHOR OF *A MORE CHRISTLIKE GOD*

"*Jesus Unbound* is a challenging and paradigm-shifting book that exposes the insidious idol worship around the Bible and persuasively points people toward the true Word of God, Jesus. While author Keith Giles deeply values the Bible, and has a profound love for it, his thought-provoking challenge is to value and love Jesus even more. Keith masterfully provides the keys to unbind our shackles of tradition and a flat reading of scripture and masterfully lures us toward a more Christ-like faith and Christ-like world. If you read *Jesus Unbound* with an open mind, and most importantly an open heart, I have no doubt you will be incredibly inspired and beautifully transformed!"

— MARK KARRIS, AUTHOR OF *DIVINE ECHOES: RECONCILING PRAYER WITH THE UNCONTROLLING LOVE OF GOD*

"Keith's books excite some and alarm others, but regardless of your reaction, one thing is for sure: Keith's books make you rethink some of your most cherished ideas. This is especially true with *Jesus Unbound*, as it challenges the most sacred cow of all, the Bible as the Word of God. This book is not the end of the matter, but another word in the ongoing conversation about the Word. So take it up and read. But most of all, think! Let Keith lead you past the book of the Bible and into a deeper relationship with Jesus, the true Word of God."

— JEREMY MYERS, AUTHOR OF *NOTHING BUT THE BLOOD OF JESUS,* AND *THE ATONEMENT OF GOD*

"Is your Christianity, Christocentric or Bibliocentric? If it's Christocentric, does that mean I don't respect the Bible? How can I know Jesus in a real, experiential way and what role does the Bible play in such a beautiful relationship? In *Jesus Unbound*, Keith Giles grapples with these questions and more like them. In the end, he points us to a Jesus that is knowable, changes our lives and—as an added bonus—gives us some interesting answers to a few thorny biblical issues. I highly recommend grappling your way through this book, because what Giles offers us in *Jesus Unbound* is nothing less than Jesus Himself."

— ROSS ROHDE, AUTHOR OF *VIRAL JESUS*

"Keith Giles has put into words what I have been trying to find a voice to for years. It won't be easy and you will—and should—struggle with some of the points laid out in this book. But at the end, we are left with a Christ-shaped hope. *Jesus Unbound* gives voice to a deeper relationship with Him in a way that is informative, logical, and based on those same scriptures."

— SETH PRICE, HOST OF *CAN I SAY THIS AT CHURCH?* PODCAST

"Keith Giles is a professional cow tipper, specializing in the sacred variety. Having toppled the sacred cow of religious nationalism in *Jesus Untangled*, he returns to the pasture in *Jesus Unbound*, where he overturns what may have become our most sacred cow of all—biblical inerrancy—along with the golden calf of biblicism that never lags far behind. But please don't imagine that Keith just likes to stir up trouble. His is such a singular focus on Jesus, the true Word of God, that he simply cannot allow such distractions to continue obstructing our view."

— CHUCK MCKNIGHT, BLOGGER AT HIPPIEHERETIC.COM

OTHER BOOKS BY THE AUTHOR

- *Jesus Untangled: Crucifying Our Politics to Pledge Allegiance to the Lamb*

- *The Power of Weakness: How God Loves to Do Extraordinary Things Through Ordinary People*

- *This Is My Body: Ekklesia As God Intended*

- *The Gospel: For Here or to Go?*

- *The Top 10 Things Every Christian Should Know (But Probably Doesn't)*

- *Nobody Follows Jesus (So Why Should You?)*

- *[Subversive Interviews] Volume 1*

- *War Is Not Christian*

- *How To Start A Ministry To The Poor In Your Own Community*

Available online at: www.KeithGiles.com

All rights reserved. No part of this book may be used or reproduced, stored in a retrieval system, or transmitted in any form or by any means, electronic, mechanical, photocopying, recording, scanning, or otherwise, without written permission from the publisher except in the case of brief quotations embodied in critical articles and reviews. Permission for wider usage of this material can be obtained through Quoir by emailing permission@quoir.com.

Copyright © 2018 by Keith Giles.

First Edition

Cover design and layout by Rafael Polendo (polendo.net)

Unless otherwise identified, all Scripture quotations in this publication are taken from the Holy Bible, New International Version®, NIV®. Copyright ©1973, 1978, 1984, 2011 by Biblica, Inc.™ Used by permission of Zondervan. All rights reserved worldwide. www.zondervan.com The "NIV" and "New International Version" are trademarks registered in the United States Patent and Trademark Office by Biblica, Inc.™

ESV Bible® (The Holy Bible, *English Standard Version*®), copyright © 2001 by Crossway Bibles, a publishing ministry of Good News Publishers. Used by permission. All rights reserved. www.crossway.org.

ISBN 978-1-938480-32-4

This volume is printed on acid free paper and meets ANSI Z39.48 standards.

Printed in the United States of America

 QUOIR

Published by Quoir
Orange, California

www.quoir.com

JESUS
UNBOUND

LIBERATING THE WORD OF GOD FROM THE BIBLE

KEITH GILES

DEDICATION

To my sons, Dylan and David.
You make me proud to be your Father.

ACKNOWLEDGEMENTS

Brian Zahnd, Brad Jersak, Steve Kline, Chuck McKnight, Rafael Polendo, Richard Jacobson, and everyone at the Mission House Church.

TABLE OF CONTENTS

FOREWORD

As modern Christians we are children of a broken home. Five centuries ago the Western church went through a bitter divorce that divided European Christians and their heirs into estranged Catholic and Protestant families. The reality that the Renaissance church was in desperate need of reformation doesn't change the fact that along with a reformation there also came an ugly split that divided the church's children between a Catholic mother and a Protestant father. In the divorce settlement (to push the metaphor a bit further) Catholic Mom got a long history, a rich tradition, and a unified church, but all Protestant Dad got was the Bible. Without history, tradition, or a magisterium, the Bible had to be everything for Protestant Dad—and Protestants have made the most of it. For five hundred years Protestant scholars and theologians have led the way in biblical translation, scholarship, and interpretation, giving the Christian world such notables as Martin Luther, John Calvin, Jacob Arminius, John Wesley, Karl Barth, C.S. Lewis, Dietrich Bonhoeffer, T.F. Torrance, Walter Brueggemann, Stanley Hauerwas, Richard Hayes, N.T. Wright, to name a few.

But with *Sola Scriptura* as a defiant battle cry there always lurked the temptation to place more weight on the Bible than it could bear, or worse yet, a temptation to deify the Bible and make an idol out of it. This has become increasingly true among the more fundamentalist clergy and congregations who are suspicious of higher education and unwilling to read their Bibles with the help of biblical scholars the caliber of Brueggemann, Hayes, and Wright. So while pretending to "take the Bible as it is," the fundamentalist reads the Bible through thick lenses of cultural, linguistic, political, and theological assumptions—interpretive lenses they are unaware of wearing.

This has led to the thoroughly modern and peculiarly Protestant problem of Biblicism. Biblicism is an interpretative method that reads the Bible as a "flat text" where every verse is itself "the word of God" and carries the same authority as any other verse. Biblicism, in effect, attempts to make the Bible the head of the church. Where Catholics err in seeking to give ultimate authority to the Pope, Protestant Biblicists err in seeking to give ultimate authority to the Bible. What Christians are supposed to confess is that Christ alone is the head of the church. The risen Christ said to his disciples, "All authority in heaven and on earth has been given unto me." With his wry British wit, N.T. Wright reminds us that Jesus did *not* say, "All authority in heaven and on earth is given unto a book you chaps are going to write." The irony of Biblicism is that for all its claims about giving final authority to the Bible, in reality Biblicism enables the individual reader to remain their own private authority. So if you don't like Jesus' explicit call to an ethic of nonviolence, you can always appeal to the wars of Joshua and David to countermand the Sermon on the Mount. This is how you use Joshua to trump Jesus. Perhaps the most clever way to ignore the commands of Christ is to cite an opposing chapter and verse. By reading the Bible as a flat text and selecting the corroborative proof-text, you can gain a biblical endorsement for nearly anything—including wars of conquest, genocide, women held as property, and the institution of slavery. This abuse of the Bible has a long and well documented history.

One of the chief problems of Biblicism is that it fails to make the vital distinction between the Bible and Christianity. Christian faith is a living tree rooted in the soil of Scripture. We cannot remove the tree from the soil in which it is rooted and expect it to survive; *but neither are we to think that the tree and the soil are the same thing!* They are not. Put simply, the Bible and Christianity are not synonymous. Yes, they are connected, but they remain distinct. Scripture is the soil; Christian faith is the living tree. They are connected, but they are *not* the same thing. So if the Bible assumes that slavery is both a tolerable and inevitable institution (see Ephesians 6:5), even explicitly stating that slaves are slaveowners' *property* (see Exodus 21:21), that doesn't mean this is the Christian ethical position on slavery. Christianity is not a slave to the Bible—Christianity is a slave to Christ! Out of the soil of Scripture grows a mature Christian faith that is not only able, but *required* to oppose all forms of slavery in the name of Jesus. Rooted in the soil of Scripture, Christianity is capable of growing an ethical branch of justice called abolition.

Since the canon of Scripture is closed, the soil of Christian faith is unchanging. But that doesn't prevent the living Christian faith itself from growing, changing, developing, and maturing over time. Of course, how it grows and changes will often be a matter of fervent debate within the church; and the deeply fractured nature of the church compounds the complexity of this problem. Nevertheless, to understand Christianity as a living tree rooted in the soil of Scripture enables the church to grow in new and redemptive ways within God's moral universe. To say that Christian faith is forever rooted in Scripture, yet distinct from Scripture, is both conservative and progressive.

Conservative in that it recognizes the inviolability of Scripture. Progressive in that it makes a vital distinction between the living faith and the historic text. But to claim that Christian faith is one and the same with the Bible is a fundamentalist mistake that is ultimately untenable. For example, I've seen Biblicists backed into a corner trying to defend the Bible by saying, "sometimes slavery is a good thing." This is Biblicism at its worst.

The ancient orthodox alternative to modern heterodox Biblicism is to say what the church has always said: Jesus Christ is the true Word of God. The Bible is the word of God, only in a penultimate sense. The Bible is the inspired, canonized witness to the Word of God who is Jesus Christ—the Word made flesh. Only Jesus Christ is the inerrant and infallible, perfect and divine Word of God. We come to accept the Bible as authoritative in the ongoing conversation about Christ that is Christian theology through the witness of Christ and the church—not the other way around. Without first appealing to Christ and then secondly to the church, we can't even account for how the Christian Bible came into being. The risen Christ commissioned the church to bear witness to the gospel throughout the world. In the course of obeying Christ's commission the church composed, collected, and canonized certain writings that became the New Testament. But we don't start with the Bible; we start with Jesus and the church. Why? Because Jesus is Lord, not the Bible. Christians worship Jesus, not the Bible. Jesus is the head of the church, not the Bible.

In reading *Jesus Unbound: How The Bible Keeps Us From Hearing the Word of God*, some readers will regard Keith Giles as controversial. I insist this is not so. Giles' approach to the Bible is not novel or modern—it's the orthodox way the Church Fathers read the Bible in the formative centuries of Christianity. It's modern fundamentalist Biblicism that should be regarded as controversial and ultimately rejected as heterodox. But I also understand that a Biblicist approach to the Bible is the default position inherited by most American evangelicals, which is precisely why Giles' book is so helpful, so timely, and so important. So as you begin your reading of *Jesus Unbound*, be assured that you are on solid ground—and keep your Bible close at hand, because as a lover of Scripture, Giles will refer to it over and over again. Both Keith Giles and *Jesus Unbound* are firmly rooted in the Bible.

– Brian Zahnd

Pastor of Word of Life Church in St. Joseph, Missouri; author of *Sinners In the Hands of a Loving God.*

"IT IS CHRIST HIMSELF, NOT THE BIBLE, WHO IS THE TRUE WORD OF GOD. THE BIBLE, READ IN THE RIGHT SPIRIT, AND WITH THE GUIDANCE OF GOOD TEACHERS, WILL BRING US TO HIM. WE MUST NOT USE THE BIBLE AS A SORT OF ENCYCLOPEDIA OUT OF WHICH TEXTS CAN BE TAKEN FOR USE AS WEAPONS."

—C.S. LEWIS

INTRODUCTION

"Jesus doesn't call us to a life of becoming progressively more and more like the Bible. Jesus calls us to a life of becoming more and more like him. The Bible is simply the vehicle to make the introduction. The goal has never been for us to live biblically. The goal has always been for us to live like Christ—and there is a massive difference between these two options."

— BENJAMIN L. COREY

Over the last few years I have noticed a strange thing about Christianity. Unlike other World religions, Christianity, in modern times, has become a movement that shares very little in common with the founder.

Where Islam demands a strict adherence to the teachings of Mohammed, and Judaism revolves around the teachings of Moses, and Buddhism is aligned directly with the teachings and practices attributed to the Buddha, Christianity seems to have very little to do with following Jesus of Nazareth.

Why is it that so many Christians have little to no expectation of following Jesus's teachings in their actual lives? For one thing, many who call themselves "Christian" today will even argue against the possibility of putting the teachings of Jesus into practice—either because to do so would be considered a "works salvation" model, or because they believe that no one could ever live up to such high standards.

Therefore, they say, we must rely solely on the unmerited Grace of God which (at least in their minds) exempts us from following any of the Messiah's commands.

But, what if Jesus really did expect us to put his words into practice? What if being a Christian is really only about being a disciple of Jesus?

NOT ONLY DO THE SCRIPTURES POINT US TO JESUS, BUT THEY PLACE HIM ALONE AT THE CENTER OF EVERYTHING. JESUS, AND ONLY JESUS, DEFINES FOR US WHO GOD IS, WHAT GOD IS LIKE, AND WHAT OUR LIVES SHOULD LOOK LIKE AS A RESULT OF THAT REVELATION.

This book will explore this question, but further than this, I hope to ask even harder questions. Like, "What if the Word of God is more than a book?" and "What if I can hear the voice of God directly, without any help from my pastor, or the Bible?"

These are challenging questions, I know. But, I believe the Scriptures themselves reveal the answers to these questions, and that what we find might surprise you.

Honestly, I am becoming convinced that the Bible is intended to teach us that the Word of God became flesh, lived among us, revealed the Father to us and now lives within every single follower of Christ at this very moment.

Not only do the Scriptures point us to Jesus, but they place Him alone at the center of everything. Jesus, and only Jesus, defines for us who God is, what God is like, and what our lives should look like as a result of that revelation.

This, I believe with all of my heart, is what Christians today need most to understand about their faith.

The ironic thing is that some of us have made the Bible an idol. We worship it. We attribute characteristics to it that should only be said of Christ.

It's as if the Word of God became flesh and dwelt among us and we have very quickly put Him back into a book again. Why? Because if the Word of God is in a book, we can manipulate, and control, and distance ourselves from Him.

Or, to put it another way: If the Word of God is alive within each and every one of us, then that means we don't need Christian pastors and teachers to explain God to us.

Quite frankly, Christians today are terrified of trusting the average person with the Spirit of the Living God. We don't really believe that the Holy Spirit within every believer can actually lead us into all truth. We doubt that His sheep can really hear the voice of the Good Shepherd. We are nervous about unleashing the Divine among the common Christian community without guard rails.

What are we so afraid of? Is it any different from when the Children of Israel drew back from the Pillar of Fire or the Cloud that spoke to them directly in the wilderness? Isn't it exactly the same as when God's people demanded a King like all the other nations and rejected God as their direct ruler? We are always seeking to put mediators and mouthpieces between ourselves and God. But God is always the One who seeks to draw near to us, to place His Spirit within us, to make His home with us and to speak directly to us as a Father speaks to His own child.

My hope with this book is to provide a fresh revelation of Christ to you and to point out how we sometimes allow good things—even the Bible—to stand between us and Him. In short, I want a Christianity that looks a lot more like Jesus.

Either our Christian faith is Christ-centered, or it is not worthy of being called "Christianity" and we should not be called "Christians."

For some, our Christianity is based upon a flat reading of the Bible where every scripture is given equal weight, regardless of who said it, why they said or who they said it to.

This "Flat Bible" approach to scripture quite often leaves Jesus and His teaching at the mercy of Moses, Elijah and the other Old Testament prophets, or even Paul and the other Apostles. The result of this is that the Messiah's commands to love our enemy become obscured by passages where God commanded violence against pagan nations; His commands to care for the poor are overridden by verses that say "if a man will not work then he shall not eat"; Jesus's prohibitions against hierarchical leadership are tempered by verses that call for believers to "submit to the authority of the Bishop"; etc.

Where does this leave us? We have a faith that takes the name of Jesus seriously, but not necessarily the commands of Jesus. We are those who call Him, "Lord, Lord" but we quite boldly do not do what He says.

As theologian Richard Rohr puts it:

"We worshipped Jesus instead of following Him on His same path… We made Jesus into a mere religion instead of a journey toward union with God and everything else. This shift made us into a religion of 'belonging and believing' instead of a religion of transformation."

And we call this "Christianity"? What if we could take a step back from all of this and reevaluate what it means to follow Christ? What if we could find a way to make sense of how we should handle verses like those above that seem to contradict Jesus and establish a simple criteria that keeps Jesus at the center of our faith?

Honestly, my own faith has undergone something of a revolution lately. I've started to look at scripture with brand new eyes. Some verses that I've read over hundreds times have suddenly taken on new meaning for me, and what I've seen cannot be unseen.

So, I'm asking you to come with me on something of a journey of discovery. If you're up for it, I'll need you to set aside your preconceived ideas about the Bible, and about how to approach the Scriptures—at least long enough to consider some of what I've seen through new eyes.

At the end you may not have arrived at the same destination that I have, but I guarantee that you will have heard something, or seen something about the Bible that you never thought about before. I also guarantee you that you will not look at your Bible, or the teachings of Jesus, in quite the same way.

Before we get started, there are few things we should establish. First, I am a Christian. I not only believe in Jesus and trust Him as my Lord and my Savior, but I hear His voice and I am abiding in Him daily.

I also believe that Jesus is fully God and fully man. I affirm the doctrine of the Trinity. I believe that the Scriptures we have today (commonly called "The Bible") are useful for teaching, reproof, correction and training in righteousness (see 2 Tim. 3:16).

Having said all of that, I do need to add that the way I view the Scriptures as a whole is probably different than the way you do. Rather than try to express that here, I will take the rest of the book to unpack what I mean and why I take the approach that I do.

But, this book is not about the Bible. Even though we will spend a lot of time talking about the Word of God and the Bible, this book is, ultimately, not about that.

This book is about Jesus. This a book about how we relate to the Bible, and to Jesus, who is the entire focus of the Bible.

We will not be pitting Jesus against the scriptures. Instead, we will explore our relationship to Jesus and examine this in light of what the Bible says about Him.

What I mean is: We often place things between ourselves and Jesus. This is called idolatry. Sometimes it can be politics, as I pointed out in my previous book *Jesus Untangled: Crucifying Our Politics To Pledge Allegiance To The Lamb*. Sometimes it can be a pastor, or a teacher, or a church that eclipses our view of Christ. Sometimes it can be our own family, or a spouse, or a job that distracts us from Jesus. Really, anything that exalts itself (or that we exalt) between us and God can become an idol in our lives.

Wait, do you mean to suggest that we can even make an idol of the Bible? Well, that is something that I will leave for you to decide for yourself by the time we reach the end of this book. For now, let's at least agree in theory that it's possible.

This might be your first real hurdle to leap as you start to read this book. If so, I apologize for introducing it so early on in the process. But I can't imagine any other way of talking about this subject without asking you to entertain the notion that, for some people, the Bible can become an idol that they worship rather than God Himself.

A few years ago, to be very honest, I would have laughed at such an idea. But in my conversations with brothers and sisters—both online and in person—I have been quite shocked to not only observe such Bible Worship, but to flat-out hear with my own ears statements like this:

- "Yes, I worship the Bible. It contains the mind and life of God."

- "I worship the Bible and you should, too!"

- "Without the Bible we could never know God or anything about Jesus."

- "Knowing doctrine and knowing Jesus are the same thing."

So, clearly, some of us in the Body of Christ are very confused about what the Bible is, and what we should worship, or not worship.

We're also very confused about Jesus and His place in our lives. Should we be following Jesus's commands or are we only expected to believe in Him and ask Him to forgive us of our sins so we can go to Heaven when we die?

What's more, many of us are very unsure of what to do with Jesus. Do we just sing to Him and pray to Him? Should we obey Him? How do we know Him? How do we learn to hear His voice? What does it mean to abide in Him as He abides in us?

This book will explore these questions and a few others. But, to be fair, a very large portion of this book will attempt to separate the Word of God from what we have come to refer to as the Bible, conceptually.

No small feat, I know. Still, my aim will be to demonstrate that Jesus is the Word of God and that the Word of God is not a book, but a person.

Not only will I try to explain the differences between the Word of God and the Bible, I will also attempt to explain why it is so important that we don't confuse our Bible with Jesus, or equate our Savior with a book about Him.

Many Christians often say that they want a more Biblical world. They cry out for our nation to return to more "Biblical" values. They hold out the Bible as the cure for everything that is wrong with our world today. They put their hope in the Holy Scriptures.

On one level I understand where they are coming from. They believe that by reading, and teaching and preaching and following the Bible, people will be saved, delivered, healed and transformed into people who are more like Jesus.

SO, RATHER THAN CRY OUT FOR A MORE BIBLICAL WORLD, I WOULD RATHER SUGGEST THAT WE CRY OUT FOR A MORE CHRIST-LIKE ONE. WHY? BECAUSE, A "BIBLICAL" WORLD ISN'T NECESSARILY A CHRIST-LIKE ONE.

The only problem with all of this is simply that the Bible never suggests anything like this. The Bible, by itself, cannot accomplish any of these things. The Bible doesn't save us. The Bible doesn't renew or refresh or restore or change us. It can't do any of those things because it is a book.

But Jesus can do all of those things. Jesus is not a book. Jesus is alive. He is God incarnate. Jesus is the Word of God made flesh that came to dwell among us. He taught us how to enter the Kingdom of God and He made a way for us to live a Kingdom life.

Jesus suffered on the cross for our sins and rose from the dead on the third day. Jesus is alive right now and He is abiding within every one of us who has surrendered to His rule and reign in their lives.

So, rather than cry out for a more Biblical world, I would rather suggest that we cry out for a more Christ-like one. Why? Because, a "Biblical" world isn't necessarily a Christ-like one. War, genocide, slavery, women-as-property and polygamy are all "Biblical" ideas. But when reevaluated in the light of Christ, such things fade into the background and are eclipsed by His radiance and glory.

No one who is strictly following the teachings of Jesus could kill other human beings for any reason, or practice slavery, or treat women as property, or justify having more than one wife, for example.

So, to me, a Christ-like world is more preferable to a Biblical world.

Does this mean I don't value the Bible? Far from it. I love the Bible. But I love Jesus so much more!

The scriptures all point us to Christ, and once we have Him, nothing else compares. In the next few chapters, I hope you will keep your eyes on Jesus as we reexamine and reconsider our assumptions about the relationship between the Bible and the Word of God.

I'm ready when you are.

CHAPTER 1

WHY I LOVE THE BIBLE

"For every ten men willing to die for the Bible, there is only one who actually reads it."

— CHARLES H. SPURGEON

I love to read. Ever since I was very young, my parents would read to me. I think that's why I love stories, and why I eventually became a writer.

When I was in elementary school, I read anything and everything I could put my hands on. My earliest favorites were Sherwood Anderson, Ambrose Bierce, and Isaac Asimov. But soon I moved on to Ian Fleming, Alistair MacLean, Alan Dean Foster, Philip K. Dick and Ray Bradbury.

One day, while visiting our pastor's house, his wife noticed I was carrying a satchel of books with me and asked me an interesting question: "Have you ever read the World's Best-Selling book?"

I stopped to consider her question and then said, "No, probably not. What is it?"

She replied: "It's an amazing old book full of adventure, danger, love, betrayal, war and redemption."

"Sounds cool," I said. "What's the title?"

Of course, she was talking about the Bible, and based on her challenge I started to read it every night before going to bed.

My routine was to lay in bed and read whatever adventure novel I was devouring at the moment and then setting that down to read at least one chapter from the Bible before I went to sleep each night.

In just over a year and a half, I had read through most of the entire Bible. Why so quickly? Because, first of all, I often read more than just one chapter, and second of all, I skipped most of Leviticus because it was just too boring.

But that was the first time I read the Bible. Later, as a Junior High student I started to read the Bible because I was helping our youth pastor to lead Bible Studies. As a High School student I was leading book studies in the Gospel of Luke (which I regretted immediately because each chapter was just a marathon to get through each week), and Isaiah (because things in the Middle East were heating up and everyone—including me—was convinced that the End Times were upon us).

In college I read through the Bible because I discovered a renewed love for Jesus at a Baptist Retreat Center in Glorietta, New Mexico. Some of the seminars and workshops I attended got me interested in Spiritual Warfare so I started studying that topic on my own.

Of course, as a college student with a minor in Philosophy I quickly encountered opposition to my dearly-held faith. A few of my professors really attacked Christianity and that sent me back to my Bible to find out if what they were saying about Jesus and the Scriptures was true or not. Because of this I started really getting into Apologetics, and Young Earth/Old Earth evidences and even put together a little four-part series of lectures about Evolution and Creation.

But all through this I read and re-read my Bible. I under-
lined. I circled. I made notes in the margins. I stuck notes all
through the Bible on folded slips of paper. I wrote references to
important verses in every blank page and white space I could
find.

Eventually that Disciple's Study Bible I bought in college
started to fall part. First the cover began to come lose. I wrapped
the spine in duct tape and kept on reading it and studying it.

A few years ago I was leading a Men's Bible Study for some
friends of mine. At the end, they took up a collection and
bought me a brand new ESV Study Bible to replace my raggedy
duct taped Bible.

Honestly, as much as I appreciate the new Bible, I still use that old
one more often because it has all
my notes and I know where to find
everything in it.

**I FELL IN LOVE—NOT
WITH THE BOOK WHICH
TOLD ME ABOUT HIM—BUT
WITH JESUS, HIMSELF!**

So, I love my Bible. I really do. If you tried to come over to
my house and take my Bible away from me, you'd have to cut my
arms off to get it out of my hands.

But, as much as I love my Bible, I love Jesus even more. A
hundred thousand million times more. See, that book told me
all about this magnificent person named Jesus who loved me and
gave Himself for me. It pointed me to a God who would rather
die than live without me. I fell in love—not with the Book which
told me about Him—but with Jesus, Himself!

I've told you about my relationship with that Book, but I
haven't mentioned my incredible relationship with Jesus: I
haven't told you about how He revealed Himself to me; how He
called me by His Spirit; how He answered my prayers; how He
worked miracles in my life; how He whispered in my ear to stop
me from getting shot dead by a prison sniper while performing

with my band at a minimum security prison; about how He healed my Dad's shattered spine and re-formed his vertebrae so he wouldn't be paralyzed; about how He provided for my family financially while I was out of work for over a year and a half (the first time) and another year the time after that; about how He fulfilled His specific promises to me during that time in ways I could have never imagined; and about how He called us to start a church where 100 percent of the offering would go to help the poor in our community; and so much more.

But if I told you about those things here in this book and your response was only to say, "Wow! What a glorious book!" you would have missed my entire point, wouldn't you?

Because what's really glorious and awesome isn't this book *about* what Jesus did for me. No, what's amazing and awesome is *Jesus* and this book only informs you of how awesome He is.

The Bible is wonderful. I do love and appreciate the Bible so very much. But my love for Jesus is so far and away greater and more precious to me than anything else in the universe that I can't even begin to compare it to anything else.

Does this mean my Bible is useless? Hardly. I will use it today and tomorrow and every day for the rest of my life. It is very useful to me.

But my relationship isn't with a book about Jesus—it's with Jesus, whom the book is about.

The New Testament really accentuates the supremacy of Jesus. For example, I love when the author of Hebrews says:

> "In the past God spoke to our ancestors through the prophets at many times and in various ways, but in these last days he has spoken to us by his Son, whom he appointed heir of all things, and through whom also he made the universe. The Son is the radiance of God's glory and the exact representation of his being, sustaining all things by his powerful word." (Hebrews 1:1-3)

Isn't that amazing? We are so blessed to be alive in a day when we can hear the voice of God's own Son. In the old days, before Jesus came, people only heard about God second-hand. They had a mediator between God and man—a prophet—who did his best to hear God's voice and then wrote or spoke what he heard to everyone else. But now—oh, Hallelujah—we have heard the voice of God through His very own Son!

Why would it be better for us to hear God's voice through His Son? Why would hearing God's voice through one of those prophets be any less remarkable?

If the testimony of those prophets was enough, then why would it have been necessary to send His Son to speak to us directly?

While you ponder this, let me ask you to consider another verse of scripture:

> "In the beginning was the Word, and the Word was with God, and the Word was God. He was with God in the beginning. Through him all things were made; without him nothing was made that has been made." (John 1:1-3)

> "The Word became flesh and made his dwelling among us. We have seen his glory, the glory of the one and only Son, who came from the Father, full of grace and truth…" (v.14)

See, there was a time, long, long ago, when God's Word was only written down on an animal skin, or bound in a book, or wrapped in a scroll. That word was limited by the human mind that heard God speak, and the human hands that wrote down those words, and the human minds that interpreted those words for us.

But when Jesus arrived that Word took on flesh and blood; that Word laughed out loud and cried tears of sorrow and joy; that Word breathed and sang and taught and healed and came alive like never before in history.

That was, and is, very significant. What does it mean for us? Well, for one thing it might mean this:

> "The Bible is not the perfect revelation of God; Jesus is. Jesus is the only perfect theology. Perfect theology is not a system of theology; perfect theology is a person. Perfect theology is not found in abstract thought; perfect theology is found in the Incarnation. Perfect theology is not a book; perfect theology is the life that Jesus lived. What the Bible does infallibly and inerrantly is point us to Jesus, just like John the Baptist did." (Brian Zahnd, *Sinners In The Hands of a Loving God*, pg. 31)

See, there were some men who wrote down what they saw this Living Word do and say, but those words about that Word are not the Word. They are still words *about* Him, and so our worship belongs to the God who is the Word—and to Him alone.

Therefore, we should be very thankful for the Bible which tells of His excellent greatness. But we should thank Him even more, for His living presence within us that testifies day and night of His enduring love for us, and that causes us to cry out "Abba! Father!"

The Word of God is alive. He is living and active and present and able to cut to the heart of our doubts and our fears.

When we read about the "Word of God" in the New Testament, this isn't usually a reference to the Bible or to scripture but to a person who is known as "The Word of God" or Jesus, the Messiah.

There are a few references where it may appear that the "word of God" is equated with the scriptures, but if we look closer—especially in light of what the Gospel of John reveals to us about the "word of God"—we'll see that the term is actually referring to Christ. Often, the term is used to describe the message of the

Gospel, but in many instances the term is used to reference a person—not a book that at that time—had not been written yet.

For example:

Then faith comes by hearing, and hearing by the *Word of God.*" (Romans 10:17)

In this verse, the "Word of God" can't mean "the Bible" because the book as we know it today it wasn't written yet. At least, not the parts being referred to here (i.e. "the Gospel").

"For the *word of God* is alive and active. Sharper than any double-edged sword, it penetrates even to dividing soul and spirit, joints and marrow; it judges the thoughts and attitudes of the heart. Nothing in all creation is hidden from God's sight. Everything is uncovered and laid bare before the eyes *of him* to whom we must give account." (Hebrews 4:11-13)

This is probably the most overly-quoted verse about the "Word of God" and it is usually referred to in the context of written passages (the Bible) instead of what it was meant to point to: a person; namely Jesus.

You see, Jesus is "alive and active". Jesus "penetrates even to dividing soul and spirit." Jesus is the one who "judges the thoughts and attitudes of the heart." A book can't do those things, not even a book as awesome as the Bible.

"I write to you, young men, because you are strong, and *the word of God* lives in you, and you have overcome the evil one." (1 John 2:13-15)

Again, the "Word of God" that lives in you and me is not a book. It's a person and that person is Jesus.

"When he opened the fifth seal, I saw under the altar the souls of those who had been slain because of *the word of God* and the testimony they had maintained." (Revelation 6:8-10)

People in the early church were not put to death because of the Bible. They were persecuted for their faith in the person of Christ, who is the Word of God.

> "He is dressed in a robe dipped in blood, and his name is *the Word of God.*" (Revelation 19:12-14)

In case there was any doubt, we are told that Jesus' name is "the Word of God." We also see that John, who writes the most about this subject, affirms that he is exiled for his faith in Jesus, not because of a book that hadn't been written yet:

> "I, John, your brother and companion in the suffering and kingdom and patient endurance that are ours in Jesus, was on the island of Patmos because of *the word of God* and the testimony of Jesus." (Revelation 1:8-10)

THE APOSTLES WANTED US TO UNDERSTAND THAT IT WAS IMPORTANT TO HAVE A RELATIONSHIP WITH A PERSON NAMED JESUS, NOT WITH A BOOK THAT THEY WERE STILL IN THE PROCESS OF WRITING DOWN.

So what? You might ask. Why does any of this matter? Here's why: because the apostles wanted us to understand that it was important to have a relationship with a person named Jesus, not with a book that they were still in the process of writing down.

Jesus even warns us not to fall in love with a book, not even with the Scriptures:

> "You search the Scriptures, because you think you will find eternal life in them. The Scriptures tell about me, but you refuse to come to me for eternal life." (John 5:39-40)

The danger that Jesus warns us about here is still very real today. We, like the Pharisees, can very easily put our hopes in the Scriptures and totally miss the Word of God who has the words of life.

Let's not forget:

- The Word of God speaks to you. The Bible is silent.

- The Word of God lives within you. The Bible is outside of you.

- The Word of God will never leave you. The Bible can be misplaced.

- The Word of God died for you. The Bible isn't alive.

- The Word of God loves you. The Bible does not.

The Word of God is a person. His name is Jesus. Get to know Him.

CHAPTER 2

A GOD LIKE JESUS

"To be a biblical Christian is not to have high views of the Bible. It is to seek and know and live the life that is depicted in the Bible."

— DALLAS WILLARD

We often want to protect and defend the deity of Christ. We insist that being a Christian means affirming that "Jesus is God."

While I agree with this, I must point out something that does not come across quite as often: the idea that *God* is like *Jesus*.

In other words, many Christians still hold fast to the notion that the Father of Jesus, as seen in the Old Testament scriptures, is a wrathful, impatient, angry and quite often bloodthirsty God. This stands in contrast to Jesus, the Son, who is a decidedly softer and more gentle and less violent personality.

On one side, this isn't surprising. There are noticeable differences in God's character between those Old and New Covenant scriptures. So, we have to reconcile those apparent contradictions somehow, and what better way than by appealing to the language of the Trinity where there are three distinct "persons" who make up the one substance we call the One True God.

Now, I'm not against the doctrine of the Trinity. I personally affirm the doctrine. But I think my fellow Trinitarians are off-base when they attribute two different personalities to the Father and the Son. Especially when the New Testament scriptures give us no wiggle room in that capacity.

Simply put: The New Testament scriptures only affirm—over and over again—that Jesus *is* what the Father looks like, and that means: The Father looks like Jesus.

Here's are a few examples from Jesus Himself:

"I and the Father are one." (John 10:30)

"Anyone who has seen me has seen the Father." (John 14:9)

"Believe me when I say that I am in the Father and the Father is in me." (John 14:11)

And here are a few scriptures from the Apostles about how Jesus and the Father are alike in heart and character:

"The Son is the radiance of God's glory and *the exact representation of his being*, sustaining all things by his powerful word." (Hebrews 1:3)

"[Jesus] Who, being in very nature God, did not consider *equality with God* something to be used to his own advantage; rather, he made himself nothing..." (Phil. 2:6-7)

"In the beginning was the Word, and the Word was with God, and *the Word was God*." (John 1:1)

"*He [Jesus] is the image of the invisible God*, the firstborn of all creation. For by him all things were created, in heaven and on earth, visible and invisible, whether thrones or dominions or rulers or authorities—all things were created through him and for him. And he is before all things, and in him all things hold together. And he is the head of the body, the church. He is the beginning, the firstborn from the dead, that in everything he might be preeminent. *For in him all the fullness of God was pleased to dwell*, and through him to reconcile to himself all things, whether on earth or in heaven, making peace by the blood of his cross." (Col. 1:15-20)

"For in him the whole fullness of deity dwells bodily, and you have been filled in him, who is the head of all rule and authority." (Col. 2:9-10)

So, what's happening here? How is it that we've gotten the wrong idea about the Father? Why do we struggle to accept that the Father is like Jesus?

Maybe it's because we're still reading those Old Testament scriptures through our old filters. Paul refers to this in 2 Cor. 3:14:

"But their minds were made dull, for *to this day the same veil remains when the old covenant is read.* It has not been removed, because *only in Christ is it taken away."*

In other words: we have a veil that covers our eyes and clouds our understanding whenever we take those Old Testament reports of the Father at face value. Those are inaccurate pictures of what our Abba is really like.

This is exactly what John intends for us to understand when he writes in the very first chapter of the Gospel of John, verse 18:

"No one has ever seen God, but the one and only Son, who is himself God and is in closest relationship with the Father, *has made him known."*

Take that in for a moment. Notice he says: *"No one has ever seen God."* That means no one—not even those Old Testament Prophets—ever really saw God clearly. This, according to the Gospel of John, is one of the main reasons why Jesus "the one and only Son" came to us: To show us who the Father *really* is.

Consider this: If everyone already had a clear picture of what the Father was like, then why would Jesus need to come and reveal Him to us? And, if this is so, then wouldn't it make sense that the picture Jesus showed us would be radically different from the foggy, murky picture we had of God before He came to show us the truth?

If you want to know what God the Father is like, what He is *really* like: Just look at Jesus.

If you want to know what the Father's attitude about you is, listen to Jesus tell the parable of the prodigal and the Father who welcomed and forgave with open arms.

If you want to know what the Father's character is really like, watch Jesus forgive those who beat him and tortured and killed him.

If you want to know what the Father does when we miss His best for us, watch as Jesus weeps over Jerusalem because they refused to know the things that are meant for peace.

In Jesus we see a Father who would rather die than live without us. We see a Father who loves us with an everlasting love. We see a Father who washes our feet, even when we betray Him.

In Jesus, we see a Father who has compassion on the outcast and the broken, and the blind, and the poor, and the prostitute, and even on those who don't worship the right way or those who have bad theology or who enrich themselves at the expense of others. In Jesus we see a Father who loves everyone who bears His image—which is every single one of us. In Jesus, we see a Father who says: "*Neither do I condemn you. Go and sin no more.*" (See John 8:11) In Jesus, we see a Father who says: "*I will never leave you or forsake you.*" (See Hebrews 13:5)

Jesus even says we should call the Father our "Abba" or our "Daddy" when we speak to Him. In fact, we're even told to pray directly to the Father—not to or through Jesus—but directly to our "Abba" Father.

"In that day you will ask nothing of me. *Truly, truly, I say to you, whatever you ask of the Father in my name, he will give it to you.* Until now you have asked nothing in my name. Ask, and you will receive, that your joy may be full…*In that day you will ask in my name, and I do not say to you that I will ask the Father on your behalf; for the Father himself loves you*, because you have loved me and have believed that I came from God." (John 16:23-27)

That means the Father is approachable. It means that He sits and waits to hear *your* voice. He has called us His children.

"See what great love the Father has lavished on us, that we should be called children of God! And that is what we are!" (1 John 3:1)

So, more and more I'm personally trying to remember that the Father is who Jesus says He is. The Father is not the wrathful, angry, violent, bloodthirsty God we read about in the Old Testament.

How do I know this? Because those people did not ever see God clearly. Only Jesus reveals the Father to us, and Jesus did not reveal to us an angry, wrathful, petty, violent God. He revealed an "Abba" to us who looks just like Jesus in heart and character.

ONLY JESUS REVEALS THE FATHER TO US, AND JESUS DID NOT REVEAL TO US AN ANGRY, WRATHFUL, PETTY, VIOLENT GOD. HE REVEALED AN "ABBA" TO US WHO LOOKS JUST LIKE JESUS IN HEART AND CHARACTER.

He revealed a God who would rather die than kill His enemies. He pointed us to a God who absorbed our violence, but refused to do any violence to us. Jesus reveals to us a God who embraces reconciliation over retaliation.

Yes, Jesus is like God, but God the Father is like Jesus. And that, my friends, is very, very good news.

JESUS IS GREATER

Throughout the Gospel of Matthew, Jesus refers to something that is "greater than" the Sabbath, the Temple, Jonah, and Solomon.

What was it? When the Pharisees asked why Jesus and His disciples broke the Sabbath, Jesus replied:

> "I tell you that something *greater than* the temple is here." (Matt. 12:6)

And then he goes on to say that he is "Lord of the Sabbath", which means that Jesus is greater than the Sabbath, as well. Later, when the Pharisees ask him for a sign, Jesus says:

> "The men of Nineveh will stand up at the judgment with this generation and condemn it; for they repented at the preaching of Jonah, and now something *greater than* Jonah is here." (Matt. 12:41)

Then, Jesus tells them this:

> "The Queen of the South will rise at the judgment with this generation and condemn it; for she came from the ends of the earth to listen to Solomon's wisdom, and now something *greater than* Solomon is here. " (Matt. 12:42)

What is greater than Solomon, or the Temple, or Jonah, or the Sabbath? It's Jesus, the promised Messiah.

Moses prophesied that the Lord would send a prophet after he was gone. He further warned that those who did not listen would be cut off from the people of Israel. (See Deut. 18:15-19) Both Stephen, and Peter reminded everyone of this in their sermons recorded in the book of Acts. (See Acts 3:22; 7:37)

When Jesus is transfigured on the mountain, he appears with Moses—who represents the Law of the Old Covenant—and with Elijah—who represents the Prophets. Peter mistakenly wants to honor all three of them equally, and then the Father removes Moses and Elijah (the Law and the Prophets) and says:

"This is my Son, whom I love; with Him I am well-pleased. Listen to Him!" (Matt. 17:5)

And when the disciples look up, only Jesus remains.

Jesus is greater than Moses. The author of Hebrews even goes so far as to say:

"Jesus has been found worthy of *greater honor* than Moses" (Heb. 3:3)

He is greater than the Old Covenant Law. Jesus is greater than the Prophets. Jesus is greater than David, and Solomon, and the Temple, and Jonah, and everyone else.

Without Jesus, no one—not even Moses, Abraham, Elijah, the Prophets or any Apostle—will ever come to the Father.

There is nothing, and no one, greater than Jesus. This is why we are told over and over again in the New Testament: Listen to Him. Obey Him. Follow Him.

As John the Baptist said:

"He must increase, but I must decrease. He who comes from above is above all. He who is of the earth belongs to the earth and speaks in an earthly way. He who comes from heaven is above all." (John 3:30-31)

LESS THAN

The New Testament also tells us that Jesus is "less than" the Father, or at least that the Father is greater than Jesus.

"You heard me say to you, 'I [Jesus] am going away, and I will come to you.' If you loved me, you would have rejoiced, because I am going to the Father, *for the Father is greater than I.*" (John 14:28)

We also know that Jesus was "made a little lower than the angels" (Hebrews 2:9) and that He "made Himself nothing, taking on the nature of a servant" (Philippians 2:6-7) which emphasizes that, while here in human form, Jesus humbled Himself.

This astounding act of humility and weakness emphasizes what Paul the Apostle refers to as "the power of weakness", where God's "power is made perfect in weakness" when we lay aside our own ability and abandon confidence in ourselves—trusting instead in the "power of Christ" which is released when we—like Christ—humble ourselves, empty ourselves, and rely completely on the Father for everything. (See 2 Cor. 12:9-10)

Just like Jesus, did, by the way. Jesus affirms that he never did anything under his own power, and that he never taught anything other than what the Father told him to say:

"These words you hear are not my own; they belong to the Father who sent me." (John 14:24)

"For I do not speak of myself, but from the Father who sent me and commanded me what I should say and what I should speak...Therefore, whatever I speak is just as the Father tells me to speak." (John 12:49-50)

"Then Jesus answered them and said, "Truly, truly, I say to you; the Son can do nothing of himself, but only does what he sees the Father do. For whatever things he [the Father] does, these are also likewise done by the Son." (John 5:19)

"Of my own self, I can do nothing. I judge only as I hear; and my judgment is just, because I do not seek my own will, but the will of the Father who has sent me." (John 5:30)

"But so that the world may know that I love the Father, I only do exactly as the Father has instructed me to do." (John 14:31)

Jesus was our role model—our blueprint if you will—for how to live a Kingdom life. Jesus was able to turn the other cheek, pray for His enemies, love those who were persecuting Him, and everything else He endured, simply because He had totally abandoned Himself to the Father in every way.

This is exactly how we are called to live the Kingdom life.

Jesus compels us to deny ourselves—our own ways of thinking and acting—and to die daily by taking up our cross and following Him, and His example, and putting His words into practice.

How can we possibly do this? Some sincerely doubt that anyone really can live the way Christ lived. But this isn't what the New Testament tells us. Quite the opposite, in fact.

When Jesus says that we can do nothing without Him, He quickly adds that we *can* bear good fruit if we abide in Him:

> "I (Jesus) am the vine; you are the branches. If you remain in me and I in you, you will bear much fruit; apart from me you can do nothing." (John 15:5)

1 Peter also affirms this:

> "His divine power has given us *everything we need* for life and godliness through our knowledge of him who called us....He has given us His very great and precious promises so that through them you may participate in the Divine nature." (1 Peter 1:3-4)

We are also told that God's amazing grace does more than merely save us from our sins, but it has enough power to help us live like Jesus did:

> "For the grace of God has appeared, bringing salvation to all men, instructing us to deny ungodliness and worldly desires and to live sensibly, righteously and godly in the present age..." (Titus 2:12)

All of this means we have no more excuses when it comes to putting His words into practice. He has shown us the way, and given us the grace to let go of our fears and trust completely in Him for everything.

EQUAL TO

It's one of the great mysteries of the New Testament, actually. How could Jesus be "the exact representation" of God and still say "the Father is greater than I am"?

GOD DID NOT SEND US A MANUAL TO READ. HE SENT US *EMMANUEL* TO BE WITH US HIMSELF AND TO RELATE TO US INDIVIDUALLY AND IN PERSON.

Part of this involves the self-limiting nature of Jesus in His incarnation. Jesus was "in very nature God" but decided to lay all of that aside to become one of us. This is when He became "less than" the Father, and even the angels. In fact, this is why the incarnation is such a miracle. The creator became the created. The unlimited willingly limited Himself. The One who lives forever took on mortality and tasted death.

So, He laid aside His Glory, and took off His great power like a robe, and humbled Himself to become a tiny embryo nestled in the womb of a poor girl in Palestine.

His identity never changed, however. He was still God, but He had taken on flesh, and thereby had wrapped Himself in a single location in space and time. This is when He became "Emmanuel" which means "God with us". This is when "the Word became flesh and dwelt among us." (John 1:14)

So, God did not send us a manual to read. He sent us *Emmanuel* to be with us Himself and to relate to us individually and in person. Remember:

> "In the beginning was the Word, and the Word was with God, and *the Word was God*." (John 1:1)

So, Jesus is equal to the Father in every way, and yet at the same time is less than the Father (in a different sense) and still greater than everything—and everyone else—in all Creation.

Meditating on these three characteristics of Jesus only makes us love Him more and fall to our knees as we begin to realize the "unsearchable riches of Christ" are more astounding than we ever imagined.

But what about those who say that the only way we know anything about Jesus or about God is through the Bible? That's what we'll explore in our next chapter.

CHAPTER 3

HOW DO WE KNOW CHRIST WITHOUT THE BIBLE?

"Christ is the original, and in him and out of him is all. He is not you, but everything that is you comes out of him. He is the One in whom you live, move, and have your being; the One who is the spark of your mind and life, the One who conceived you from everlasting...Christ is the living animating force of reality and is unveiling himself within all, summoning space and time and all consciousness forward to the fulfillment of love."

— JACOB M. WRIGHT

In the ongoing conversation about the identity of the "Word of God" and differences between the Bible and Christ, we often hear reactions that sound something like this:

> "You cannot know Christ apart from the scriptures. Unless He is a figment of your own imagination, then of course He can look and say anything you like. Everything we know about Christ comes to us from the Bible."

That sounds right, doesn't it? I mean, how else could we know anything about God or about Jesus apart from the Bible?

But, is that what the Bible says? Do the Scriptures affirm this idea that we cannot know Christ apart from the Bible?

As we look deeper we run across verses that suggest something a lot more breath-taking than what we might have expected.

For example, as we've already seen, the Gospel of John tells us that "The Word of God became flesh and dwelt among us" (John 1:14) and that this same Word of God is Jesus (John 1:1) and now Jesus (the Word of God) lives within every one of us who abides in Him (John 15:4).

SO, IF THE WORD OF GOD IS JESUS, AND IF JESUS NOW LIVES WITHIN ME, THEN I HAVE THE WORD OF GOD INSIDE OF ME. MAYBE THIS MEANS THAT WE CAN KNOW CHRIST THE WAY WE KNOW OUR OWN VOICE, OR OUR OWN HEARTBEAT, BECAUSE HE IS ALIVE WITHIN US.

So, if the Word of God is Jesus, and if Jesus now lives within me, then I have the Word of God inside of me. Maybe this means that we can know Christ the way we know our own voice, or our own heartbeat, because He is alive within us.

The Scriptures also tell us that we "have the mind of Christ" (1 Cor. 2:16) right now and that we can discern "the things that come from the Spirit of God…because they are discerned only through the Spirit" (1 Cor. 2:15) and this Spirit is now alive within us.

Jesus also affirms to us that we can hear His voice and that He, as the Good Shepherd, is more than capable of making Himself heard:

"I am the Good Shepherd and my sheep hear my voice" (See John 1:1-16)

So, not only can we all hear our Master's voice individually, we are also empowered by the Holy Spirit who "leads us into all truth" (John 16:13), as Jesus promised us.

This statement from Jesus cannot mean that we hear His voice only through the scriptures. Especially since none of his words would have been canonized for another few hundred years.

Clearly, Jesus intends for us to understand that He will speak to us by His Spirit and that we are all capable of hearing His voice.

The Apostles also affirmed these same ideas by pointing to the evidence of the Holy Spirit within us as proof that we belong to Christ and that we can know the truth apart from anything else:

> "As for you, the anointing which you received from Him abides in you, and you have no need for anyone to teach you; but as His anointing teaches you about all things, and is true and is not a lie, and just as it has taught you, you abide in Him." (1 John 2:27)

> "And in the last days it shall be, God declares,
> that I will pour out my Spirit on all flesh,
> and your sons and your daughters shall prophesy,
>   and your young men shall see visions,
>   and your old men shall dream dreams;
> even on my male servants and female servants
>   in those days I will pour out my Spirit, and they shall prophesy."
> (Acts 2:17-18)

The anointing every Christian has received is from the Holy Spirit and this anointing teaches us about all things.

But, does all of this mean we don't need the Bible? Far from it. Why wouldn't we avail ourselves of the all the treasures provided for us in the scriptures?

But my point is this: According to the Bible, we can know God, and Christ, by the indwelling Spirit of the Living God within us.

This is what the Bible teaches us about how we primarily know God and Christ and the Truth: By the Spirit of God.

So, according to the Bible, everything we know about Christ comes from Christ. Yes, some of the information we have does come from the Bible, (and that of course comes from Christ, too), but even more wisdom and truth is available to us directly from the One who lives and breathes within us on a daily basis. This is more than mere information about God, it is the direct experience of God and with God.

I think that's worth at least one big "Hallelujah!" Don't you?

Are you ready for a little more excitement? This is all exactly what the New Covenant is all about.

> "Behold, the days are coming," declares the Lord, "when I will make a new covenant with the house of Israel and with the house of Judah…this is the covenant which I will make with the house of Israel after those days," declares the Lord, *"I will put My law within them and on their heart I will write it;* and I will be their God, and they shall be My people. *They will not teach again, each man his neighbor and each man his brother, saying, 'Know the Lord,' for they will all know Me, from the least of them to the greatest of them,"* declares the Lord, "for I will forgive their iniquity, and their sin I will remember no more." (Jeremiah 31:31-34)

Notice that the result of this New Covenant would be that God's people would not turn to teachers for wisdom about God because "My law (will be) within them and on their heart I will write it" and because "they will all know me, from the least of them to the greatest of them".

When these words were written it probably sounded like science fiction. How could God do this? What would it be like to have God's Law written on our hearts? What would it be like not to depend on teachers to know God? How amazing would it be if everyone who belonged to God knew Him so intimately?

Now, today, because of Christ's accomplishment and fulfillment of the Law and the Prophets, the Holy Spirit has been poured out on all flesh. We, right now, are those people that Jeremiah prophesied about. We are the people who now have God's Law written on our hearts. We are the people who are now empowered by the Spirit of the Living God to "Know the Lord" because we can all know Him, "from the least to the greatest."

Isn't that great news? How sad would it be to live in such a time as this and not take advantage of such a wonderful gift from God?

Jesus declared this New Covenant in His blood. We remember this New Covenant every time we eat the bread and drink the cup. Why stop there? Why not continue onward to claim the promises that come with this New Covenant reality? Why not listen for the voice of our Good Shepherd and learn to "Know the Lord" in this one-on-one way?

In fact, if we don't live this way, we are actually choosing to live an Old Covenant life and to embrace and Old Covenant kind of faith rather than a truly Christ-centered one that leads us to grace and truth.

Jesus was quick to remind us that we have no need of any other teacher except Him:

> "Nor are you to be called instructors, for you have one Instructor, the Messiah" (Matt. 23:10)

Please don't miss this, my friends. It is for freedom that Christ has set you free from the Old Covenant kind of life. The opportunity to know God intimately and to hear the voice of Jesus directly is wide open to you now. As my friend Brant Hansen said: "I'm so glad the Creator gave us more than a book, a collection of rules, or lonely positive energy. He gave us a Person."

The renowned theologian Richard Rohr also reminds us:

> "For those who are willing to see, the divine self-revelation of creation as image and likeness is everywhere evident, long before Scriptures were written. God was not mute for 14 billion

years. Even though Abraham didn't have the Bible (either of the Testaments!), he and Sarah still knew God—which is true for all the Patriarchs and their families. They instead knew God by the relationship called faith, better translated as "trust in goodness."[1]

What does it mean to "know the Lord"? What is the significance of this knowledge? Is it merely about having the right information? Or is it something much, much more? That's what our next chapter is all about.

CHAPTER 4

THE GOSPEL: INFORMATION OR TRANSFORMATION?

"We have millions and millions of Christians who have had no experience of God, and the Church, for the most part, prefers it that way. We can then supply beliefs and dogmas as a replacement for encountering a living God. This is part of the reason so many people cling to the Bible or their theological beliefs so firmly. Because, to them, it is the closest thing to God they have ever encountered."

— MARK VAN STEENWYCK

Knowing God is pretty important. In fact, according to Jesus, knowing God *is* eternal life. As He says here:

> "Now this is eternal life: to know God and His Son whom you have sent." (John 17:3)

But is this "knowing" a reference to gaining the right information about God? Is it about having knowledge? Or is it something more than that?

Many Christians honestly do believe that having all the right information about God is essential to our salvation. For them, the greatest heresy would be to believe the wrong things about

God. This is also why they cannot bear to be around others who hold different beliefs than they do. If having the right information is what the Christian faith is all about, then having wrong information is the worst sin of all.

But that's not what Jesus is talking about here. Not at all. The word Jesus uses here for "to know" in the Greek is "*ginosko*"; a word which maps to the same word used in the Hebrew scriptures for the way a husband "knew" his wife in a deeply intimate, sexual way.

In other words, this "knowing" is less like studying for a test and more like connecting with someone on a physical, spiritual and emotional level. The shocking thing is that the person we are urged to "know" in this way is God Himself.

To "know God and His Son" like this, therefore, involves an ongoing, daily relationship with Him that many would consider a little bit scandalous.

Nevertheless, we are expected to have an intimacy with God that conceives something within us, and that "something" is new life.

This means that knowing God is more about transformation than information. Here's something else about knowing God that you might find interesting:

> "…No one knows the Father except the Son and those to whom the Son chooses to reveal him." (Matt. 11:27)

So, the best way to know Father God is to get to know Jesus, and the best way to know Jesus is to listen to His voice, spend time with Him and start putting His words into practice.

Let me ask you: Do you think of the Gospel as being more about having the right information about God? Or do you see it as being more about the transformation we experience as we learn to abide in Christ?

You might be tempted to think that it's both, or that it really doesn't matter how you think of the Gospel, but I believe it matters a great deal.

For example, if we think of the Gospel as mainly information, then we become lawyers and modern Pharisees who argue semantics and debate doctrine. Salvation is seen as having the right information - the right beliefs and doctrines, in the right order. Those who have different information than we do are heretics. Those who accept our information are "saved" and those who don't are either not truly Christians or their salvation is in question.

But Jesus speaks of a Gospel that is based on an intimate relationship with himself. He talks about the Gospel as being primarily about transformation, not mere information.

He proclaims the Good News (Gospel) of the Kingdom by urging everyone to "think different" (*Metanoia* in the Greek; usually translated as "Repent!" in most English translations).

He points out that it's impossible for a bad tree to produce good fruit and that if you don't first "make the tree good" you'll never produce good fruit.

Through the Gospel, Jesus makes us good trees who can produce the good fruit of righteousness which is pleasing to God. (See Matt. 12:33)

Jesus says that life in the Kingdom comes when we "know God and the Christ whom He has sent" (John 17:3) That word translated "know" is not about information. It's the same word used to say that "Adam 'knew' Eve" and that involves an intimacy; a way of knowing that conceives new life within.

So, we are called to "know God" and to "know Christ" in an intimate way that conceives a new life within us - the new life of the Kingdom that comes only as we abide in Him and He abides in us.

That's a relationship where we are daily learning to love Him more as we come to "know this love that surpasses knowledge" and become "filled to the measure of all the fullness of God." (Eph. 3:19)

If the Gospel is merely information, then we don't need a relationship with a living person who transforms us. Just give me the information and I'll study it and memorize it and enforce the proper communication of that information.

> SEE, IF CHRISTIANITY IS ABOUT BEING RIGHT THEN IT'S EASIER TO JUSTIFY CUTTING OFF THOSE PEOPLE YOU DON'T AGREE WITH. BECAUSE, IF YOU SEE CHRISTIANITY AS A QUEST FOR "RIGHTNESS," THEN BEING WRONG IS THE GREATEST SIN OF ALL.

But if the Gospel is about a transforming relationship with a vibrant, fantastic being of light and love, then we will certainly receive information about Him, but this will go far beyond mere data and exponentially transcend human knowledge to explode into an intimacy that conceives something new within.

Jesus wants to change us. He wants us to become more like himself. We should desire that, too. The way we are transformed into His image is to immerse ourselves in Him and surrender ourselves completely to Him so that He can make us into the good trees that bear good fruit.

> "Beloved, we are God's children now, and what we will be has not yet appeared; but we know that when he appears we shall be like him, because we shall see him as he is." (1 Jn. 3:2)

Another problem with thinking of the Gospel as having the right information is that it can lead us to value being right over and above the command to love others as Jesus has loved us.

See, if Christianity is about being right then it's easier to justify cutting off those people you don't agree with. Because, if you see Christianity as a quest for "rightness," then being wrong is the greatest sin of all.

However, if you see Christianity as following Jesus, then being right is less important than the quality of your relationship with Him.

Relationships are messy. They're not about correctness, or accuracy. No one measures their relationships in such terms. Instead, we gauge the health of our relationships based on how open our communication is, and how honest we can be with one another, and how much time we spend together.

Jesus quite often equates our love for Him with how well we love one another. If we love one another as He has loved us, then we are loving Him by our obedience, and by being obedient we are loving others, too.

> "A new commandment I give to you, that you love one another: just as I have loved you, you also are to love one another. By this all people will know that you are my disciples, if you have love for one another." (John 13:24-25)

Elsewhere, Jesus connects our horizontal relationships with others to our vertical one towards God. He tells us that we should go and reconcile with our brother before we return to complete our acts of worship. (See Matt. 5:23-24) And the Apostle John pushes it further by saying that if we claim to love God but don't love our brothers and sisters, we're just liars. (See 1 John 4:20)

So, what should we learn from this? Perhaps that our interpersonal relationships don't need to hinge on agreement with one another. I can love someone who has the wrong ideas about doctrine. I can fellowship with a brother or sister who sees things differently than I do. I can even extend grace to someone who calls me a heretic.

But, what if they have wrong ideas about God? Maybe they do have a few wrong ideas about God. But, perhaps we are the ones who are off base? Until we know for sure, our main goal should be to love one another as Christ has loved us. Remember, "Love covers a multitude of sins." (1 Peter 4:8)

In the early church, for example, there were three different views of the doctrine of hell. For over 300 years Christians held wildly divergent views of the afterlife without feeling the need to convince everyone they were right and others were wrong. It was only after Constantine shifted the paradigm of Christianity from a focus on Christ-likeness (orthopraxy) to one of Correctness (orthodoxy) that Christians started persecuting one another over differences of opinion in matters of doctrine.

Nowhere are we taught in scripture that the Gospel is about having the correct information. Instead, we're taught that it's about having a transformational relationship with Jesus. This relationship involves abiding in Christ as He abides in us. Through this process, our sinful self is daily crucified and our spiritual self—"a new creature"—is brought to life within us.

It's a constant exchange of death for life where the resurrection power of Christ is increasingly revealed in us and transforms us into people who are like Him.

But, what about sound doctrine? Aren't we told to stand for what's right in the scriptures?

Usually, this idea of "sound doctrine" happens to mirror a denominational statement of faith ratified years ago and enforced by church leadership, (deacons, elders, etc.), and reinforced through church membership classes and sometimes even Sunday School classes.

But, here's what Paul had to say about "sound doctrine" when he wrote to the apostle, Titus:

> "You, [Titus] however, must teach what is appropriate to sound doctrine." (Titus 2:1)

See? Obviously Paul knew that it was very important to teach sound doctrine in the Church. Luckily for us, Paul breaks down the elements of this sound doctrine for us here:

> "Teach the older men to be temperate, worthy of respect, self-controlled, and sound in faith, in love and in endurance. Likewise, teach the older women to be reverent in the way they live, not to be slanderers or addicted to much wine, but to teach what is good. Then they can urge the younger women to love their husbands and children, to be self-controlled and pure, to be busy at home, to be kind, and to be subject to their husbands, so that no one will malign the word of God." (Titus 2:2-5)

Wait. So, Paul says that sound doctrine is all about being self-controlled, loving, patient and full of faith? You may have been expecting a list of rules and laws to follow. Let's see what he says next. Maybe the rules and laws come later:

> "Similarly, encourage the young men to be self-controlled. In everything set them an example by doing what is good. In your teaching show integrity, seriousness and soundness of speech that cannot be condemned, so that those who oppose you may be ashamed because they have nothing bad to say about us." (Titus 2:6-8)

So, according to Paul, sound doctrine seems to be more about how we live our lives before one another; things like setting examples for one another by doing good, showing integrity, speaking truthfully, living a simple, decent life before men. That's shocking, isn't it? So is the next part:

> "Teach slaves to be subject to their masters in everything, to try to please them, not to talk back to them, and not to steal from them, but to show that they can be fully trusted, so that in every way they will make the teaching about God our Savior attractive." (Titus 2:9-11)

Ok, then. So, slaves should continue to serve their masters in humility, show that they can be fully trusted and in so doing,

"they will make the teaching about God our Savior attractive."
Wow. Paul's goal here seems to be more about living out a sin-
cere, authentic faith before the world and less about a set of
belief statements. Maybe he gets to teaching about speaking in
tongues or the pre-millennial kingdom in this last part?

> "For the grace of God has appeared that offers salvation to all
> people. It teaches us to say "No" to ungodliness and worldly
> passions, and to live self-controlled, upright and godly lives
> in this present age, while we wait for the blessed hope—the
> appearing of the glory of our great God and Savior, Jesus Christ,
> who gave himself for us to redeem us from all wickedness and
> to purify for himself a people that are his very own, eager to do
> what is good." (Titus 2:11-14)

Whoa. Now Paul has started to jack up the whole idea of
grace too. Here we see once again where Paul says that grace
teaches us to say "no" to ungodliness and worldly passions. Some
teach that God's grace is there to give us a pass when we say
"yes" to our worldly passions. But, Paul seems to teach here that
grace empowers us to live out the sound doctrine of living self-
controlled, upright and godly lives.

Paul ends by saying:

> "These, then, are the things you should teach." (Titus 2:15)

"Sound doctrine" as Paul outlines it for us here involves
teaching one another to live simple, humble, godly lives of service, love, compassion and integrity before one another and to
the world around us. How? By the power of grace that "teaches
us to say 'no' to ungodliness and worldly passions."

If our churches today would major on sound doctrine like
this and not divide over foolish disagreements about the return
of Christ, or doctrines of tongues or the rapture, or predestina-
tion, or any other topic, we might actually live out true sound
doctrine as Paul describes.

Disputes over doctrines come because we allow them to become more important to us than our unity in Christ. But, what is it that makes us one? Christ! Not our agreements about infant baptism, or freewill, or pre-millennialism, or the King James Bible. None of that. The only thing that makes us one is Christ.

So, in summary, if the Gospel is about having the right information, then being right is everything. But, if the Gospel is about transformation, then being Christ-like is everything.

We have to let go of the need to "be right" and begin to embrace the reality of Christ's transformational life.

> **IF THE GOSPEL IS ABOUT HAVING THE RIGHT INFORMATION, THEN BEING RIGHT IS EVERYTHING. BUT, IF THE GOSPEL IS ABOUT TRANSFORMATION, THEN BEING CHRIST-LIKE IS EVERYTHING.**

We're all in process. None of us is right about everything. Thankfully, we don't need to be. We just have to keep abiding in Him.

One of my favorite quotes comes from a letter written by a 15th Century Bishop named Fenelon who gave some wonderful advice to someone he was mentoring in Christ. He said:

> "If you stopped learning today you wouldn't live long enough to put into practice all that you already know." (Fenelon, *Let Go*)

This quote has stuck with me for a long time now. I believe it's true. For most of us, the time for learning new information about Jesus is long over. It's way past the time for putting into practice what we already know that Jesus commanded us to do.

Sadly, most of us would rather continue to read and learn and study, and then re-learn and re-study, and take lots of notes until Jesus comes back.

But Jesus isn't coming back for people who know stuff about Him. That's why He said: "Why do you call me 'Lord, lord' and do not do what I command?" (Luke 6:46) That's why He also said: "Now that you know these things, you will be blessed if you do them." (John 13:17)

Because what Jesus wants us to understand is that having the information about the Gospel is worthless if you do not obey the Gospel.

In other words, it's not how much information about Jesus we have. It's what we do with that information once we have it.

The great Christian philosopher, Soren Kierkegaard put it this way:

> "The Bible is very easy to understand. But we Christians are a bunch of scheming swindlers. We pretend to be unable to understand it because we know very well that the minute we understand, we are obliged to act accordingly."

Ultimately, it's not about what you or I do, anyway. The point is not for us to "live a life for Jesus". That's honestly impossible. What Jesus wants us to do is to stop trying to live for Him and start allowing Him to live in us.

Until Jesus is alive in you - living and breathing within - you are not alive anyway. Remember, Jesus told us: "Apart from me you can do nothing" (John 15:5)

And we are told that "Whoever has the Son has life; whoever does not have the Son of God, does not have life." (1 John 5:12)

So, let's not ask ourselves "What can I do for God?" but instead, let's ask, "What could God accomplish through me if I was totally and completely surrendered to Him?"

That's the Gospel of the Kingdom: One life, totally surrendered to His rule and reign.

Can we take that step? Can we begin, right now, to let Jesus have His way with us? Can we lay down our lives and let Him live in us by His Spirit?

Honestly, that's what Jesus came and died for: *all* of you! Not just a little piece of you, but every single part; even (and especially) that part of yourself that you are most afraid of surrendering to Him.

He is trustworthy. He won't mess up your life. Instead, He will give you real, abundant life, starting the moment you let go of this one, which in reality is no real "life" at all.

> "For whoever wishes to save his life will lose it; but whoever loses his life for my sake will find it. For what will it profit a man if he gains the whole world and forfeits his soul? Or what will a man give in exchange for his soul?" (Matt. 16:25-26)

Let's consider for a moment what we have learned so far about Jesus and how He reveals the Father to us:

- Jesus is the "Word of God" who took on flesh in the incarnation and came to dwell among us as "Emmanuel" (literally "God with us").

- Jesus is the exact representation of the Father.

- All the fullness of the Godhead exists in Christ in bodily form.

- In the past, God spoke to us through the prophets, but in these last days He has spoken to us directly through His Son.

- No one has ever seen God at any time—not the authors of the Law or the Prophets in the Old Testament—but only Jesus has seen God, because He is God and He came from God.

- Jesus came to reveal the Father to us.

- Jesus said that if we have seen Him then we have seen the Father.

- Jesus said that we have one teacher and that He alone is that teacher.

- Paul tells us that, to this day, a veil covers our eyes whenever we read the old testament scriptures and that only in Christ is it taken away.

- Jesus said that He was the Way, the Truth and the Life and that no one will ever come to see or to know the Father except through Him.

So, what does all of this have to do with how we should read the Scriptures? Everything. That's what we'll explore in our next chapter.

CHAPTER 5

READING SCRIPTURE THROUGH THE LENS OF CHRIST

"Human beings are 'God-breathed,' yet nobody claims we are 'inerrant.' Yet, somehow the Bible we wrote is both?"

— MATTHEW J. DISTEFANO

At the end of the previous chapter we recapped a long list of things about Jesus that speak to the way He is our key to understanding who God is, what God is like and how we should read the Old Testament scriptures.

This is how the New Testament authors, and even Jesus Himself, defines what it means when we refer to Christ as the "Word of God."

Jesus begins His ministry by teaching His disciples from the Sermon on the Mount where He quite boldly contrasted His teachings with the teachings of Moses, saying:

"You have heard that it was said...but I say to you..." (Matt. 5:38)

Try to understand how radical it would be if someone came to your church and said, *"You have heard someone say 'Love one another as I have loved you', but I say to you 'Just love people who love you in return.'"*

Hopefully there would be a huge gasp from the congregation at the audacity of this person to stand up in front of everyone and contradict the words of Jesus. Who does he think he is? What authority does he have to correct the teachings of Christ?

But this is exactly the same kind of statement that Jesus makes when He quotes from Moses and then corrects that teaching with one of His own.

This is also why the people are astonished and whisper to one another at the end of His Sermon about the way He taught.

> "And when Jesus finished these sayings, the crowds were astonished at his teaching, for he was teaching them as one who had authority, and not as their scribes." (Matt. 7:28-29)

Indeed, the authority that Jesus taught with was impressive. He corrected the words of Moses and gave new and more stringent conditions for entering the Kingdom of God, even suggesting that his disciples needed to have a righteousness that surpassed the Pharisees.

This is significant, because it points out what we have already learned from Hebrews 1:1-3, that, at one time, God spoke to us through prophets, but now He has spoken to us through His own Son.

And still today God speaks to us—not merely through the Bible—but through His own Son. Jesus is what God is saying to us in these last days. In the past He spoke to us through the Old Testament, but now, God's message to us is found in Christ.

Remember, Jesus promised us that He would speak to us and that we could hear His voice. Remember that Jesus promised to send us the Holy Spirit who would live within us and would lead us into all truth.

He even said that it was *better for us* that He went away so that He could send us the Spirit who could abide within us and teach us the Words of God, which He would write on our hearts.

Remember also that we have one mediator between God and us and that this mediator is Christ.

"For there is one God and one mediator between God and mankind, the man Christ Jesus…" (1 Tim. 2:5)

Our mediator is Christ. Not your pastor. Not your church. Not your denomination. Not your bishops, or elders, or deacons. Only Jesus is our mediator. Only Jesus stands between you and God. Only Jesus connects you to God. Only Jesus reveals who the Father is, and what the Father is like.

So, no one—and nothing—else stands between you and God. Not even the Bible.

This is what the Bible teaches us: Jesus is our mediator and Jesus is alive within us and we can hear His voice.

THIS MEANS THAT ANY SCRIPTURES THAT DO NOT ALIGN WITH WHAT HAS BEEN REVEALED TO US IN CHRIST ARE NOT THE WHOLE TRUTH.

We are also told by Jesus Himself that we have one instructor. Who is it?

"For you have one instructor—the Messiah." (Matt. 23:10)

Jesus is our instructor. He teaches us. He leads us into all Truth by His indwelling Holy Spirit.

Jesus tells us that He is the Way, and the Truth and the Life. (John 14:6)

This means that any scriptures that do not align with what has been revealed to us in Christ are not the whole Truth.

This is our mandate now, from Moses and even from God the Father Himself—"Listen to Jesus!"

This means we need to read the Bible through the lens of Christ if we ever hope to know who God is and what God is really like.

Why else would Paul tell us that *"to this day a veil covers [our] eyes whenever the Old Testament scriptures are read and only in Christ is it taken away"* if this were not the case? (See 2. Cor. 3:14)

Because, without Christ as our lens, or filter, we cannot properly understand what is truth and what is error. But now that we have seen and known Jesus, we truly "see the Father" and we recognize the "Truth" when we see it because Jesus has shown us the "Way" to see the Father clearly.

Therefore, nothing is true unless it lines up with the revelation of Christ. Nothing points the way to God unless it aligns with the teachings of Jesus. Nothing contains the words of life unless those words correspond to the words spoken by Jesus.

As Peter exclaimed:

"Where else can we go, Lord? You have the words of life" (John 6:68)

And as Jesus reminded us:

"You search the scriptures because you think that in them you have eternal life; and yet you refuse to come to me that you may have life." (John 4:39-40)

And as John tells us:

"He who has the Son has life, but he who does not have the Son of God does not have life." (1 Jn. 5:12)

In the same way that without Christ we have no life, it could be said that without Christ we have no truth about God either. His unique access to the Father was one of the central claims of His Messianic ministry, as we have already referenced here.

Jesus is the Father's preferred method of speaking to us in these last days. Not through prophets or teachers, not even through apostles or pastors, but through His Son.

Does this mean we should ignore those prophets, teachers, apostles and pastors? Of course not. But what it does mean is that if those prophets, teachers, apostles and pastors say something about God that disagrees with what Jesus has already told us or revealed to us, we must hold tight to the teachings of Christ.

For many, this is where they warn us about being deceived, or remind us how easy it is to fall into error. As if our best and only safeguard against error or deception is to be found in the security of holy men rather than in the absolute authority of Christ and His Holy Spirit that lives within us.

Let us not fool ourselves. These fear-based warnings are more about a desire to maintain control over people in the Church—to ensure they don't question the doctrines of the denomination or challenge the teaching of the pastor in the pulpit.

This is why you will never hear sermons about the priesthood of all believers, or the passages about how the average Christian is capable of hearing the voice of God apart from the approved mediators. To empower the people of God in this way is to effectively dismantle the clergy class and calls into question the entire status quo of traditional Christianity which is built upon coercion and control.

So, we are told to question our ability to hear God's voice. We are told to doubt that still small voice. We're warned not to trust our own discernment. All of this keeps the Holy Spirit of God at a safe distance from the people, only to be handled by the trained professionals in the seminaries. It also, ironically, contradicts the scriptures.

As some New Testament scholars have observed:

"We came up with the idea of inerrancy because we needed another mediator between God and man other than Jesus." (T.F. Torrance)[1]

"It's a very Western certainty. I mean, we don't even have the original manuscripts in order to create [or justify] a certainty out of, yet we've come up with a doctrine that we can be certain of rather than a relationship that we can be certain of...So, what are we putting our certainty in: the character and nature of a God we are in relationship with, or the certainty of hermeneutical extrapolation that is without encounter?" (William Paul Young)[2]

How do you know if your own church community has bought into this fear of the Holy Spirit? It's simple enough to determine. Just try to start a Bible study in your own home and invite some of your friends. See how long it takes for someone to question your ability to lead such a study by yourself. See if anyone demands to see your notes or expects you to ask permission from the leadership first.

I experienced something like this at a church I was serving at over a decade ago. A few college students wanted to start a Bible study in their dorm room with some friends. They were told they could not host this study without one of the pastors leading it, and so they cancelled it.

This astounded me. How could we refuse to allow these twenty-something students to gather and read the words of Jesus together? It was their decision. It was their dorm room. What right did anyone have to tell them they were not qualified to handle the words of Jesus without a professional clergy in the room with them?

We often act as if the Gospel and the Scriptures are too dangerous to be handled by mere mortals. As if the most likely outcome of allowing everyday people to read the Bible would result in confusion and false doctrine, not wisdom, insight and freedom.

Let's look at what the New Testament says about all of this:

"I myself am convinced, my brethren, that you yourselves are full of goodness, complete in knowledge and competent to instruct one another." (Romans 15:14)

"For you can all prophesy in turn so that everyone may be instructed and encouraged." (1 Corinthians 14:31)

What I find fascinating is that, according to Jesus and the Apostles, every believer is capable of hearing the voice of God, and yet, in today's modern church we typically find that only one, or perhaps a few, are expected to hear God's voice and communicate His will to the Body.

Why is that? Partly because we have embraced a false Clergy-Laity divide which suggests that only those who have attended seminary or graduated from Bible College are capable of hearing God's voice or instructing the Body.

As one New Testament scholar, Howard Snyder, put it:

"The clergy-laity dichotomy is…a throwback to the Old Testament priesthood. It is one of the principal obstacles to the church effectively being God's agent of the kingdom today because it creates a false idea that only 'holy men,' namely, ordained ministers, are really qualified and responsible for leadership and significant ministry. In the New Testament there are functional distinctions between various kinds of ministries but no hierarchical division between clergy and laity. The New Testament teaches us that the church is a community in which all are gifted and all have ministry."[3]

Essentially, in spite of the fact that the veil in the temple was torn in two when Christ said "it is finished," we have virtually re-sewn the veil and re-instituted our own system of professional priesthood.

I would like to suggest that it is time for another reformation within the Body of Christ. One where we demolish the clergy-laity distinctions and empower every member to listen for the still, small voice of God.

It's also very important for us to spend time reading the words of Jesus ourselves. This process isn't accomplished in a vacuum. We need to know what Jesus says and we need to become familiar with what He taught. How else can we call ourselves His followers? How can we possibly do what He says if we don't know what He said?

IF WE NEVER STEP OUTSIDE OUR COMFORT ZONES AND MOVE DEEPER INTO AN INTIMATE RELATIONSHIP WITH JESUS, WE'LL NEVER LEARN TO RECOGNIZE WHEN HE SPEAKS.

This doesn't mean that everyone has the gift of teaching. We still need to rely on one another and trust the Spirit of Christ that is alive in our community of faith to lead us. We need to pray for, and start to develop our gift of discernment. We need to test the Spirits and hold tightly to the words of Jesus, trusting in His Spirit to guide us.

Everyone who is under the care of the Great Shepherd can hear Him speak. We need to learn to trust Him to do that, and we need to learn to trust ourselves—and especially His Spirit within us—to discern His voice.

Like any skill, this may take time to develop. But if we never step outside our comfort zones and move deeper into an intimate relationship with Jesus, we'll never learn to recognize when He speaks.

What we often forget is that learning and teaching in the Body of Christ isn't merely an academic process. It's not the same as taking a class on Trigonometry or how to speak Chinese. In those cases, it is necessary to have a teacher—an expert in the field—who fully understands the material and has an ability to communicate the necessary information to everyone else. But in the Church, we are not only gathering to understand information about God, are we? Instead, when we gather together the author Himself is always in the room with us. The main character is close at hand to answer any questions and explain everything to us.

> "For where two or three come together in my name, there am I with them." (Matthew 18:20)

> "If any of you lacks wisdom, he should ask God, who gives generously to all without finding fault, and it will be given to him." (James 1:5)

Can I give you a personal testimony of how God spoke to my wife, Wendy and I at a time when we lacked wisdom?

Around 9:45 p.m. one Sunday night, our doorbell rang. On our doorstep was one of our neighbors standing with her arm around a teenage girl who had a cut over her eye which was bleeding slightly. The girl's name was Angelica. She had just run away from a girl's home which was a few blocks away from where we lived. Angelica had broken through a screened window and tripped on the curb outside in her escape, which is how she had cut her face. Unsure of where to go, she had just started running through the streets, praying to God, "Where should I go, Lord? Help me!"

That's when she ran up to our neighbor's house and knocked on the door. When Tammy, our neighbor, opened the door, Angelica said, "Please don't call the police," and then told her what had happened.

Seeing this scared young girl on her doorstep, Tammy said, "I know a pastor and his wife down the street. They'll know what to do."

That's when they knocked on our door. We had just put our boys to bed and had settled down after a stressful week of airport drama, sickness, and seemingly endless Holy Week preparations which included hosting a Passover Seder, an interactive Good Friday service, and of course, Easter Sunday in the park that very morning.

Honestly, Wendy and I wanted nothing more in that moment than to go to bed and sleep for days. But as we listened to Angelica share her story, our hearts were desperate to help her.

Tammy turned to Angelica and said, "I know you don't know me, but I trust these people with all my heart and I know that they will take care of you."

Angelica nodded her head and quickly repeated, "Please, just don't call the police, OK?"

After Tammy left we brought Angelica inside and sat her down on the sofa. Wendy and I sat on the floor near her and just asked her to tell us her story. She was in tears a lot of the time, but eventually she got her story out.

At first, she wanted us to drive her to her Mom's house in Anaheim. "What's the phone number?" Wendy asked. But Angelica didn't know the number, she only knew the address.

I took a second to let that sink in. This teenage girl was in a stranger's house on Easter Sunday night. She had nowhere to go. No friends to call on. Even her own Mother, just a few miles away, was probably part of why she was in this girl's home in the first place. My heart broke for her.

"Angie?," I said. "I don't know your situation. But I'm guessing that your Mom's house is probably not a very safe place for you. Is it?"

She hung her head and nodded. "You're right," she said.

I asked her to consider returning to the Girl's Home, since she had affirmed that the people there were really nice and very supportive of her. But, she completely refused to go back.

"What do you want to do?" Wendy asked.

"I want to go back to Orangewood," she said. This was another children's home that she had stayed at previously.

"We can't just drive you over there and drop you off, can we?" She shook her head.

"My social worker said she can help me on Tuesday," she said.

"OK," I said, "but by Tuesday everyone is going to know you ran away, including your social worker. By then, they won't take you to Orangewood, they'll take you back to where you ran away from, or maybe to Juvenile Hall for running away." I saw that she realized I was right.

"Can I just stay here?" she asked.

"Sure, you can stay here," Wendy said. "But the police are going to be looking for you. People are going to be worried about you, and you won't get to go back to Orangewood if you're a runaway."

We tried calling her social worker, but she didn't answer. We got a recording that said she would be back in the office on Tuesday.

So, that's when we decided to pray for wisdom. We all three held hands and bowed our heads and we asked God to honor His promise that if anyone lacks wisdom they can ask Him. So, that's exactly what we did.

We confessed that we didn't know what to do to help Angelica, but that we knew that God had a plan that was the best for her life. We prayed and then we waited.

God was faithful. He gave Wendy the answer. She looked up at me after we said "Amen" and said, "I think we should call Orangewood."

I wasn't getting it. "No one is going to answer," I said. "It's 10 p.m. on Easter Sunday evening. Who's going to be there?"

Wendy just repeated: "I think we should just call over there and see."

So, I begrudgingly looked up the phone number and dialed it, fully expecting to say, "See? I told you no one would be there," but then a live voice said, "Hello?"

So, I explained that I was trying to help a runaway girl. The woman on the phone asked me the name of the girl. "Angelica," I said. That's when the woman said, "Oh, I know Angelica! Let me talk with her."

Dumbfounded, I handed the phone over and the two of them talked for about ten minutes. Turns out the woman working the phones that night used to be Angelica's case worker.

Eventually, they made a deal: Angelica promised to go back to the girl's home for one more night and her former caseworker promised to find a way to readmit her to Orangewood. Angelica handed me back my phone. About twenty minutes later, a van pulled up in front of our house and they took Angelica back to the girl's home, safe and sound.

Now, I want you to know that if God had not told us what to do that night, Wendy and I would never have thought to call Orangewood. Before we prayed together and asked God for wisdom, neither of us had any clue about what we should do. But, once we prayed and asked God to tell us what to do, He answered us.

I could tell you a few more stories like that, but hopefully you get the point. God really does give us wisdom if we will ask Him for it. He really does speak to us by His Holy Spirit.

So, to put it in another context, even if the people who have the gift of teaching are not present for one of our church services, it's still possible for everyone else in the room to read the Scriptures, and pray, and ask God for wisdom and insight. If we do this, we should expect to receive revelation from God Himself through the Holy Spirit.

In this way, the Church is never without a teacher. The expert we require is always present because He is alive within us.

Again, this doesn't make everyone in the room a teacher, but everyone in the room does have access to hear the Teacher and to share what they learn from Him with one another.

So, it's still possible for everyone in the Body to come together under the Headship of Christ and share the gifts they've received from the Holy Spirit and participate in the life of Jesus together.

We have the living God within us. He is our instructor. Don't you think it's time we got busy listening to Him?

CHAPTER 6

KNOWING THE TRUTH

"Christ is the sole 'tuning fork' with which all Scripture must resonate."

— RICHARD MURRAY

When Jesus said, "I am the Way, the Truth and the Life and no one comes to the Father except through me," He wasn't talking about how we get to heaven after we die.

In context, Jesus was telling His disciples that He was going away and that He was going to prepare a place for us to be with Him. We often read those words as being about heaven, and the phrase "In my Father's house are many rooms" (v.2) as a reference to our heavenly mansions where we expect to spend eternity.

But Jesus never uses the term "My Father's house" to refer to Heaven. Instead, that term is most often used to refer to the Temple of God. For example, when Jesus cleared the Temple He said, "You have made my Father's house into a den of thieves" and that wasn't a reference to Heaven but to the Temple.

Now, we know that the Temple of God is actually another way of referring to the Body of Christ, or the Church. So, what

Jesus is really saying is that He is going away to prepare the Church (His Body) to become a place where He and the Father make their home with us. This is exactly what Jesus says later in the same chapter:

> "If anyone loves me, he will keep my word, and my Father will love him, and we will come to him and make our home with him." (John 14:23)

After telling His disciples that He is going away to prepare the Church to become a place where He and the Father can meet with all of us, He says:

> "And you know the way to where I am going." (John 14:4)

To which, Thomas replies:

> "Lord, we do not know where you are going. How can we know the way?" (John 14:5)

Now, where did Jesus say He was going? To prepare a place where He and the Father could be with us. (see v. 3) Jesus responds to Thomas by saying:

> "I am the way, and the truth, and the life. No one comes to the Father except through me." (John 14:6)

So, in the context of the entire conversation, Jesus is talking about how we come to the Father. This is more than a statement about something that will happen after we die. The context tells us that we can come to the Father, through Jesus, right here and now.

So, let's look at the next thing Jesus says:

> "If you had known me, you would have known my Father also. From now on you do know him and have seen him." (John 14:7)

The "from now on" part is clearly supporting the idea that Jesus is talking about something that we can experience now, not just after we are dead. Next, Philip says:

"Lord, show us the Father, and it is enough for us." (John 14:8)

Here is where Jesus takes the opportunity to stress something very important:

"Have I been with you so long, and you still do not know me, Philip? Whoever has seen me has seen the Father. How can you say, 'Show us the Father'? Do you not believe that I am in the Father and the Father is in me? The words that I say to you I do not speak on my own authority, but the Father who dwells in me does his works. Believe me that I am in the Father and the Father is in me, or else believe on account of the works themselves." (John 14:8-11)

So, here's what we need to understand: Jesus is the Truth about God. He is the Way to the Father and through Jesus we can fully see and understand what the Father is really like.

Or, to put it another way, if Jesus is the way to see and know the Father, then anything that doesn't agree with Him about the Father is not true. This means we have to start with Jesus. We have to know Him and abide in Him. If we abide in Him, then He will abide in us, and as Jesus promised us, He and the Father would both come to make their home in us.

As Jesus and the Father come to live in us by the indwelling Holy Spirit, we are empowered to hear His voice and we can read the scriptures through the lens of Christ.

Let's go back and look at a few scriptures from the New Testament that very specifically identify Jesus as our one-and-only source for knowing who God is and what God is like.

Before we look at those verses, let me ask you to notice a few things:

First, notice that in nearly every case Jesus is either explicitly contrasted with the Old Testament Prophets, or it is implicitly suggested that He is the superior source for information about who God is and what God is like.

> **WHENEVER THE NEW TESTAMENT SAYS SOMETHING ABOUT JESUS, IT DOESN'T AFFIRM THAT THE OLD TESTAMENT WAS RIGHT AND JESUS CONFIRMED IT. INSTEAD, IT OFTEN EITHER IGNORES WHAT THE OLD TESTAMENT CLAIMS OR FLAT-OUT CONTRADICTS IT.**

Secondly, please notice that whenever the New Testament says something about Jesus, it doesn't affirm that the Old Testament was right and Jesus confirmed it. Instead, it often either ignores what the Old Testament claims or flat-out contradicts it.

This is pretty significant, really. Because it's not as if the authors of the New Testament were ignorant about what the Old Testament said about God. Yet, their claims about Jesus very intentionally supersede those made by the Law and the Prophets.

To help you see this, I will point out examples of how these explicit and implicit contrasts are made between Jesus and the Old Testament prophets, just in case they are not obvious. This will also give us an opportunity to review some of what we've learned so far.

Ready? OK, here we go.

According to the New Testament:

Who does God speak to us through today?

(Not Moses. Not Elijah.)

Jesus.

"In the past God spoke to our ancestors through the prophets at many times and in various ways, but in these last days he has spoken to us by his Son, whom he appointed heir of all things, and through whom also he made the universe. The Son is the radiance of God's glory and the exact representation of his being, sustaining all things by his powerful word." (Hebrews 1:1–3)

Who is the one mediator between God and man?

(Not the Law. Not the Prophets.)

Jesus.

"For there is one God and one mediator between God and mankind, the man Christ Jesus…" (1 Tim. 2:5)

Who is the one instructor who teaches us?

(Not the Law. Not the Prophets.)

Jesus.

"For you have one instructor – the Messiah." (Matt. 23:10)

Who is the one we should listen to?

(Not Moses. Not Elijah.)

Jesus.

*After removing Moses (the Law) and Elijah (the Prophets), God says: "This is my Son. Listen to Him!" (Matt. 17:4-6)

Who is the only one who removes the veil that covers the Old Testament scriptures?

Only Jesus.

"For to this day, when they read the old covenant, that same veil remains unlifted, because only through Christ is it taken away. Yes, to this day whenever Moses is read a veil lies over their hearts. But when one turns to the Lord, the veil is removed." (2 Cor. 3:14-16)

Where is the one place we can go to find life?

(Not to the scriptures.)

Jesus.

"You search the scriptures because you think that in them you have eternal life; and yet you refuse to come to me that you may have life." (John 4:39-40)

Who is the only one who has ever seen God at any time?

(Not Moses. Not Elijah.)

Jesus.

"No one has ever seen God, but God, the one and only [Jesus] makes Him known." (John 1:17-18)

Who is the "Word of God"?

(Not your Bible.)

Jesus.

"In the beginning was the Word and the Word was with God and the Word was God...and the Word became flesh and dwelt among us." (John 1:1; 14)

Who reveals the Truth to us about the Father?

No one but Jesus.

"Whoever has seen me has seen the Father." (John 14:9)

"Jesus said to him, "I am the way, and the truth, and the life. No one comes to the Father except through me. If you had known me, you would have known my Father also." (John 14:6-7)

"No one knows who the Father is except the Son and those to whom the Son chooses to reveal him." (Luke 10:22)

Please note in these scriptures above how easy it would have been for the New Testament writers to affirm the Old Testament and exalt Jesus at the same time. *But that's not what they do.*

For example, in John 1:17-18, if the author had intended to protect the witness of the Old Testament prophets who claimed they saw God and wanted to affirm their testimony about God's character, how easy it would have been to say something like this:

"Whereas Moses and Elijah had also seen God in the past, Jesus came from God as the Word made flesh to confirm their testimony."

But, what he wrote sounds nothing like that. Not at all. It says this:

"No one has ever seen God, but God, the one and only [Jesus] makes Him known." (John 1:17-18)

That's pretty harsh. It's almost as if John is trying to make a point here. He wants to say that, until Jesus came, we did not have an accurate revelation about who God was and what God was like.

Let's think of it another way: Let's say that John wanted to communicate to us that Jesus's testimony about the Father was accurate but the testimony of the Old Testament Prophets was inaccurate. How might he do that? Maybe he would say something like:

"No one except Jesus has seen the Father. Jesus came to reveal the Father to us because our ideas about God were less than exact."

Or...he might say it like this:

"No one has ever seen God at any time, but God, the one and only [Jesus] makes Him known." (John 1:17-18)

Now, we shouldn't assume that John was just using hyperbole or that he had a momentary lapse of memory. Clearly, he was aware that people in the past, like Moses and Elijah, had claimed to see God and to hear from Him. That's why his statement is so radical: *"No one has ever seen God..."*

The same could be said for every other verse above. If the authors had wanted to affirm the Old Testament, they had every opportunity to do so. Instead, they very boldly contrast Jesus with the Law and the Prophets and emphasize the supremacy of Christ.

Now, before you break out the pitchforks let me say that I do believe the Law and the Prophets point us to Christ. In fact, they do that beautifully. We should be very grateful for the Old Testament scriptures that foreshadow the coming of Jesus.

Jesus Himself said that He did not come to abolish the Law and the Prophets but to fulfill them, and this is exactly what He did. (Matthew 5:17-18; John 17:4; John 19:30)

Because of this fulfillment, those scriptures have become obsolete and are fading away. (Hebrews 8:13; 2 Cor. 3:7-11)

What we have now is the Living Word who is alive inside us. (John 14:23; John 15:4)

He has written His law on our hearts. This is what the new covenant is all about. (Jeremiah 31:31; Hebrews 8:10-12)

So, if anyone is to blame for pitting Jesus against Moses or Elijah, or the Old Testament scriptures, it's Paul, Matthew, John and the author of Hebrews.

What the New Testament teaches us is that Jesus is the standard. He is the plumb line for who God is, and what God is like. Jesus is the Truth and anything that doesn't agree with Jesus is not the Truth.

> "For the law was given through Moses, but grace and truth came through Jesus Christ." (John 1:17)

Have you ever wondered why Jesus didn't write the New Testament or the Gospels personally? Wouldn't that have once and for all eliminated any arguments about scripture being inerrant and perfect?

Perhaps that is exactly why Jesus didn't write it personally. Maybe He depended upon human beings who would share their understandings with us so that we would have no other choice but to discern their meaning for ourselves, question their motives, weigh their judgment, and test everything they said by the Holy Spirit.

Isn't this exactly why Jesus told us that it was better for us if He went away; so that He could send us the Holy Spirit who would lead us into all Truth? (See John 16:13)

If the goal was to hand us a text that could never be questioned, then Jesus Himself could have penned every word and handed it to the Apostles. But He did not do that. Instead, He allowed them to write down what they remembered, and even to disagree with one another about what exactly happened, and when, and how. He allows us to read those words today with the guidance of the same Holy Spirit who speaks to us and reveals truth to us. He allows us to dialog with one another over what we understand and what we don't understand.

> AS ALWAYS, JESUS IS COMFORTABLE WITH OUR QUESTIONS. HE WANTS US TO WORK IT OUT. HE TRUSTS US TO WRESTLE WITH THE UNKNOWN AND TO DIG OUT THE ANSWERS ONE AT A TIME. HE IS NOT TROUBLED BY UNANSWERED QUESTIONS, EITHER.

As always, Jesus is comfortable with our questions. He wants us to work it out. He trusts us to wrestle with the unknown and to dig out the answers one at a time. He is not troubled by unanswered questions, either. Jesus was asked dozens of questions during His earthly ministry and not only did He leave most of them unanswered, he usually responded with a few questions of His own; many of which also went unanswered.

We, unfortunately, are a people who are obsessed with answers. We want to "know" the truth. We want everything spelled out for us. We want a formula, but the trouble is, once we have a formula we don't need God anymore, do we?

See, God wants us to lean on Him. He wants us to come to Him to have life, not to a book. God wants us to admit that we don't have it all figured out by coming to Him with our questions and inquiring of Him for wisdom.

Our problem is, we don't like to look foolish. We also don't want to be wrong. We don't want people to think we're not smart, or that we don't have it all figured out.

But the truth is, we are not so smart. We do not have all the answers. There are many great mysteries of Christ that we do not yet understand.

God is OK with our questions. He is not troubled by our lack of wisdom, but He is concerned about our abundance of pride. Those who receive grace from God are the humble, not the proud. Remember:

> "God opposes the proud, but gives grace to the humble." (James 4:6)

"IN OUR FOOLISH ATTEMPTS TO DEFEND THE FAITH, WE HAVE TURNED THE SCRIPTURES INTO A SOLID PIECE OF CEMENT AND BLOCKED THE DOORWAY TO LIFE WITH IT...THE BIBLE IS MANY WONDERFUL THINGS, BUT IT IS NOT THE WORD OF GOD—ONLY THE FATHER'S BELOVED SON IS.

WHEN THAT LIVING WORD IS REDEFINED BY MEN AS WORDS ON A PAGE, THEY MURDER THE PROPHETS OF EVERY AGE, FROM ADAM DOWN TO THE PRESENT, BLOCKING THE HOLY SPIRIT FROM THEIR OWN HEARTS AS THEY DENY HIS VOICE CAN BE HEARD IN ANYONE ELSE'S. AND HIS VOICE IS HEARD BY ANYONE WHO WILL LISTEN."

—DON FRANCISCO

CHAPTER 7

THE INVISIBLE MAN AND HIS SHADOW
(AN ALLEGORY BY CHUCK MCKNIGHT)

There once was an invisible man. Though no one could see this man, they could see his shadow. Over the years, people tried to learn about the man by observing his shadow. They recorded their findings, carefully documenting every detail they saw in the shadow.

But they ran into some problems. For one thing, the shadow didn't always look the same to everyone. It would acquire the color and texture of whatever it happened to be resting on. And it seemed to change shape depending on the time of day and the angle from which people observed it.

Some saw the shadow as extraordinarily tall and skinny, while others saw it as short and squat.

Furthermore, people couldn't always tell what the man behind the shadow was doing. Wherever the shadow went, things seemed to happen; strange and mysterious things; horrible and wonderful things. But because the observers could not determine the man's actions from the shadow, they tended to assume that he had caused all of these things.

Through it all, the observers documented the shadow, just as each of them saw it. And they documented the things that happened when

*the shadow was nearby. Though their descriptions sometimes dif-
fered, they all accurately described what they had seen in the shadow.*

*Then one day, the man became visible. He appeared to the people
and walked their streets in full sight. Now they could see who he
really was. Much of what they had seen in the shadow was true of
the man. Yet, understandably, much was also different.*

*Some of his observers rejoiced to see the man clearly. With their
new knowledge about the man, they went back through their docu-
mentation, and they finally understood what he had been doing all
along. Furthermore, they documented the man himself so that those
who had not seen him in person could know what he was really like.*

*But others had made a critical mistake. They forgot that they were
looking at a shadow. They came to believe that the shadow itself was
the full revelation of the man. And so, when the man appeared, they
rejected him. "This man looks nothing like our shadow," they said.
"After all, we can still see the shadow right there on the ground."*

*They could not understand that the shadow merely pointed to
the man.*

*Much time has passed since the man appeared. Today, he is not
visible in the way he once was. But his observers left us with two distinct records. The first describes his shadow. And the second describes
the man himself. Both records provide accurate descriptions, but they
must be properly understood.*

*Some interpreters of these records still cling to the shadow, and
thus they reject the man. Others accept the man, but only in as much
as he looks like his shadow. They are happy that he became visible,
but they still believe that the shadow was a better representation of
him. So they reinterpret the man to make him match his shadow.*

*But the shadow has only ever pointed to the man. The man him-
self is the only perfect revelation. And we must interpret the shadow
in his light.*[1]

As this allegory illustrates so beautifully, the Hebrew prophets wrote down what they thought God was like and how they assumed God must behave based on their limited experience of Him. At times God did clearly speak to them and gave them divine insight about Himself. Those verses were most clearly represented by Messianic prophecies that foretold of One to come who would fulfill the Law and establish God's everlasting Kingdom on earth.

These breathtaking passages speak of Jesus with such clarity and vividness that we can hardly believe that they were written hundreds of years before the incarnation of Christ.

For example:

"They pierced my hands and my feet. I can count all my bones. They look, they stare at me; They divide my garments among them, And for my clothing they cast lots." (Psalm 22:16-18)

"For a child will be born to us, a son will be given to us; And the government will rest on His shoulders; And His name will be called Wonderful Counselor, Mighty God, Eternal Father, Prince of Peace." (Isaiah 9:6)

"'Thus says the Lord of hosts, "Behold, a man [Y'Shua or Joshua] whose name is the Branch [a common term for Messiah], for He will branch out from where He is; and He will build the temple of the Lord." (Zechariah 6:12)

"Rejoice greatly, O daughter of Zion! Shout in triumph, O daughter of Jerusalem! Behold, your king is coming to you; He is just and endowed with salvation, Humble, and mounted on a donkey, Even on a colt, the foal of a donkey." (Zechariah 9:10)

"And I will pour out on the house of David and the inhabitants of Jerusalem a spirit of grace and pleas for mercy, so that, when they look on me, on him whom they have pierced, they shall mourn for him, as one mourns for an only child, and weep bitterly over him, as one weeps over a firstborn." (Zechariah 12:10)

"But he was wounded for our transgressions, he was bruised for our iniquities: the chastisement of our peace was upon him, and with his stripes we are healed." (Isaiah 53:5)

These verses, and many others like them, are scattered all throughout the Hebrew scripture. They are unmistakably accurate windows into the future Messiah who would come and fulfill the promises of God and usher in the everlasting Kingdom of God.

In these examples we see the invisible man's shadow in sharp detail so that when He appears before us in the flesh, we have no doubt who we are looking at.

But for every one of these glimpses of clarity, we have many more portrayals of God that do not resemble the reality that was revealed to us in Christ. In those cases we see a sharp contrast, even a contradiction, of the God that Jesus demonstrated to us in the flesh.

For example:

"Now go, attack the Amalekites and totally destroy all that belongs to them. Do not spare them; put to death men and women, children and infants, cattle and sheep, camels and donkeys." (1 Sam. 15:3)

"So now, kill all the male children and kill every woman who has had sexual relations with a man, but keep alive for yourselves all the young females who have not had sexual relations." (Numbers 31:17-18)

"Then they devoted all in the city to destruction, both men and women, young and old, oxen, sheep, and donkeys, with the edge of the sword." (Josh. 6:21)

"When Israel had finished killing all the inhabitants of Ai in the open wilderness where they pursued them, and all of them to the very last had fallen by the edge of the sword, all Israel returned to Ai and struck it down with the edge of the sword. And all who fell that day, both men and women, were 12,000, all the people of Ai. But Joshua did not draw back his hand with which he stretched out the javelin until he had devoted all the inhabitants of Ai to destruction." (Josh. 8:24-26)

If Jesus is the "exact representation of God" (Hebrews 1:3) and if Jesus came to reveal the Father to us because "no one has ever seen God" (John 1:18), and if Jesus says that anyone who has seen Him has seen the Father (John 14:9), then we have to ask ourselves if Jesus would have ever commanded anyone to slaughter women and children like this.

> WHAT WE SEE IN JESUS IS AN ABBA FATHER WHO GATHERS CHILDREN TO HIMSELF, WHO HONORS WOMEN AND WHO COMMANDS HIS PEOPLE TO LOVE THEIR ENEMIES. IT WOULD BE VERY INCONSISTENT FOR JESUS TO CALL FOR THE SLAUGHTER OF THOUSANDS OF WOMEN AND CHILDREN.

What we see in Jesus is an Abba Father who gathers children to Himself, who honors women and who commands His people to love their enemies. It would be very inconsistent for Jesus to call for the slaughter of thousands of women and children.

Jesus says that it is the Enemy who has "come to steal, kill and destroy" but that He gives us life. (John 10:10)

Several times in the New Testament the teachings of Moses are described as those which bring death and they are contrasted with the testimony of Jesus which brings us life.

> "For the law was given through Moses; grace and truth came through Jesus Christ." (John 1:17)

> "He has made us competent as ministers of a new covenant—not of the letter but of the Spirit; for the letter kills, but the Spirit gives life. Now if the ministry that brought death, which was engraved in letters on stone, came with glory…will not the ministry of the Spirit be even more glorious?" (2 Cor. 3:6-8)

"For if those who depend on the law are heirs, faith means nothing and the promise is worthless, because the law brings wrath."
(Romans 4:14-15)

"…through Christ Jesus the law of the Spirit who gives life has
set you free from the law of sin and death." (Romans 8:2)

So, what are we to say about those scriptures in the Old
Testament that portray God as a bloodthirsty, vengeful warrior
who commands genocide? Was God once an angry deity who
took delight in the murder of children? Or, perhaps what we
have in these verses is a picture of what God looks like through
a veil? In Christ, the veil is removed and we can see clearly that
God is not the one who sanctified the slaughter of women and
children after all. Instead, we have an example of what happens
when people project their own desires onto God and justify their
own violence by assuming that God approves of it.

Let's look at this problem another way: What if you heard the
Lord speak to you in your quiet time with Him and He clearly
told you to go next door and kill your neighbors, taking special
care to eliminate their daughter and their newborn infant son,
and also their pets. Would you stop and wonder if that was really
God's voice? Would you almost instantly reject such thoughts as
coming, not from Jesus, but from the Enemy who came to steal,
kill and destroy?

If so, then why wouldn't that same level of discernment help
you to make a similar assessment of God's supposed commands
to kill women and children in the Old Testament? If Jesus would
not command His disciples to rip unborn children out of their
mother's wombs, then neither did Father God. Those scriptures
that place those words in God's mouth are mistaken and are
projections of what those writers believed God wanted them to
do, but they were wrong. How do we know this? Because when

the Word becomes flesh and dwells among us, He tells us what the Father is like, and it's not anything like the wrathful God portrayed in those passages.

What about when the Old Testament writers claim that God does not want the sick or the handicapped coming near Him or His sanctuary?

> "And the Lord spoke to Moses, saying, 'Speak to Aaron, saying, None of your offspring throughout their generations who has a blemish may approach to offer the bread of his God. For no one who has a blemish shall draw near, a man blind or lame, or one who has a mutilated face or a limb too long, or a man who has an injured foot or an injured hand, or a hunchback or a dwarf or a man with a defect in his sight or an itching disease or scabs or crushed testicles. No man of the offspring of Aaron the priest who has a blemish shall come near to offer the Lord's food offerings; since he has a blemish, he shall not come near to offer the bread of his God. He may eat the bread of his God, both of the most holy and of the holy things, but he shall not go through the veil or approach the altar, because he has a blemish, that he may not profane my sanctuaries, for I am the Lord who sanctifies them." (Lev. 21:18-23)

Does any of this sound like Jesus? Or, do we see Jesus drawing near to the lame and the blind, and healing the handicapped, and removing all their diseases? So, which of these pictures of the Father is the most accurate? Do we really believe that God was once squeamish about the sick and the deformed, but later on changed His mind and opened His heart to them?

God is either unable to make up His mind about those with deformities and sickness, or He has always loved all of His children regardless of their physical condition or appearance.

Jesus decisively settles the question for us. He shows us that God is love, and that He is not about dividing us from one another, or from Himself at all. In Christ, we see a Father God who is not offended by our deformity but is full of compassion for everyone.

There are also passages in the Old Testament that suggest that God is too holy to look upon our sins and that He must turn His eyes away from us. For example:

> "Your eyes are too pure to look on evil, and You cannot tolerate wrongdoing." (Habakkuk 1:13)

> "But your iniquities have made a separation between you and your God, and your sins have hidden His face from you so that He does not hear." (Isaiah 59:2)

But, does this line up with what we see when we look at Jesus? No really. In fact, if anything Jesus was criticized for spending too much time with sinners:

> "The Son of Man has come eating and drinking, and you say, 'Behold, a gluttonous man and a drunkard, a friend of tax collectors and sinners!'" (Luke 7:34)

WHERE MANY OF US HAVE GOTTEN CONFUSED IS WHEN WE ASSUME THAT THE OLD TESTAMENT SCRIPTURES ARE A SINGLE, UNBROKEN, UNANIMOUS VOICE. INSTEAD, WHAT WE NEED TO REALIZE IS THAT THE SCRIPTURES ARE A COLLECTION OF VOICES HAVING A DIALOG WITH ONE ANOTHER ABOUT WHO GOD IS AND WHAT GOD IS LIKE.

To be fair, those two Old Testament passages above which appear to say that God is too Holy to look upon sin, or that our sins have hidden His face from us, are not saying this at all. Simply continue reading a few verses further and, in both cases, you'll see that God *does* look upon those who sin, and He *does* see those who are doing unrighteous things. But, even so, Jesus is still our final word on the matter. We look at Jesus and we see clearly that God not only looks at sinners, He loves them and is willing to do whatever it takes to bring them nearer to Himself, even if it kills Him.

Where many of us have gotten confused is when we assume that the Old Testament scriptures are a single, unbroken, unanimous voice. Instead, what we need to realize is that the scriptures are a collection of voices having a dialog with one another about who God is and what God is like.

For example, Moses says that God requires animal sacrifice and gives very detailed instructions about how and when to conduct these sacrifices.

> "Now this is the law of the guilt offering; it is most holy. In the place where they slay the burnt offering they are to slay the guilt offering, and he shall sprinkle its blood around on the altar. Then he shall offer from it all its fat: the fat tail and the fat that covers the entrails, and the two kidneys with the fat that is on them, which is on the loins, and the lobe on the liver he shall remove with the kidneys. The priest shall offer them up in smoke on the altar as an offering by fire to the LORD; it is a guilt offering." (Lev. 7:1-5)

This sort of detailed instruction goes on for quite a long time in Leviticus. But, later on, David says that God doesn't desire a sacrifice at all.

> "You do not delight in sacrifice, or I would bring it; you do not take pleasure in burnt offerings." (Psalm 51:6)

> "Sacrifice and offering you did not desire—but my ears you have opened—burnt offerings and sin offerings you did not require." (Psalm 40:6)

This is a direct contradiction to what was said by Moses in Leviticus. But the prophet Jeremiah confirms what David says and repeats the notion that God never commanded anyone to sacrifice animals.

> "Thus says the LORD of hosts, the God of Israel, "...For I did not speak to your fathers, or command them in the day that I brought them out of the land of Egypt, concerning burnt offerings and sacrifices. But this is what I commanded them, saying,

'Obey My voice, and I will be your God, and you will be My people; and you will walk in all the way which I command you, that it may be well with you.'" (Jeremiah 7:21-23)

The prophet Hosea continues this same narrative and adds:

"For I desire steadfast love and not sacrifice, and the knowledge of God rather than burnt offerings." (Hosea 6:6)

Finally, Jesus shows up quoting Hosea—not Moses—affirming the notion that animal sacrifice wasn't the Father's idea.

"(Jesus said) Go and learn what this means: 'I desire mercy, and not sacrifice.' For I came not to call the righteous, but sinners." (Matt. 9:13)

To cap it all off, the author of Hebrews also says:

"For it is impossible for the blood of bulls and goats to take away sins. Consequently, when Christ came into the world, he said, 'Sacrifices and offerings you have not desired, but a body have you prepared for me; in burnt offerings and sin offerings you have taken no pleasure. Then I said, 'Behold, I have come to do your will, O God, as it is written of me in the scroll of the book.'" (Hebrews 10:4-7)

This is just one example of how ideas are developed throughout the scriptures over time. One prophet says something, another adds or subtracts or modifies that idea, and yet another offers a different angle. But it is Christ who has the final say. He is our standard. He is our best source for Truth.

So, once we accept the fact that the Bible is a collection of insights, ideas and, yes, inspiration, about the nature of God, we can start to realize why it's so necessary for us to take hold of Christ and view the scriptures through Him. Because without Jesus, we simply have no assurance of who was right about God, or what God is really like.

Speaking of the Scriptures, Bible Scholar Thomas Torrance had this to say:

"[T]he extraordinary fact about the Bible is that in the hands of God it is the instrument he uses to convey to us his revelation and reconciliation, and yet it belongs to the very sphere where redemption is necessary.

"The Bible stands above us speaking to us the Word of God and yet the Bible belongs to history which comes under the judgment of God and requires the cleansing and atoning activity of the Cross.

"When we hear the Word of God in the Bible, therefore, we hear it in such a way that the human word of Holy Scripture bows under the divine judgment, for that is part of its function in the communication of divine revelation and reconciliation.

"Considered merely in itself it is imperfect and inadequate, and its text may be faulty and errant, but it is precisely in its imperfection and inadequacy and faultiness and errancy that God's inerrant Holy Word has laid hold of it that it may serve his reconciling revelation and the inerrant communication of his Truth.

"Therefore the Bible has to be heard as Word of God within the ambiguity of its poverty and riches, its weakness and power, and heard in such a way that we acknowledge that in itself in its human expression, the Bible comprises the word of man with all the limitations and imperfection of human flesh, in order to allow the human expression to fulfill its divinely appointed and holy function for us, in pointing beyond itself, to what it is not in itself, but to what God has marvelously made it to be in the adoption of his Grace.

"The Bible itself will pass away with this world, but the Word of God which it has been inspired to convey to us does not pass away but endures forever."[2]

Our insistence upon an inerrant and infallible scripture is part of what prevents us from fully embracing the Word of God, who is a living person dwelling within each of us by His Spirit.

By clinging to a Book that cannot be questioned, (although it is filled with contradictions, errors and flaws), we have constructed a version of Christianity that is built upon a foundation of wood, hay and stubble; a foundation that cannot stand the test of criticism or even logic.

What we should be doing is admitting that our Scriptures may be less than perfect, but our foundation, our "Cornerstone" if you will, is solid and firm. Of course, this is Christ, not a religious book.

The Scriptures never hold themselves up to be our foundation. The Bible never claims to be our rock. Instead, they point us to God, and especially to Christ, who is our strong tower, and our precious cornerstone.

If we truly follow the Scriptures, they will inevitably point us to Christ. What we do next is what really matters most. Either we will remain safely comfortable in the arms of the Bible, or we will take that step of uncomfortable faith and fall into the arms of the One who loved us and gave Himself up for us on the Cross.

CHAPTER 8

NEW COVENANT CHRISTIANITY

"What I don't understand, frankly, is the people who say they love the Bible but refuse to take it seriously...who refuse to see it for what it is, who reject historical criticism, who fail to consider social and historical context and the real lives of the human authors and communities that gave them birth. Using the Bible as a magic book, claiming it is without any human error or human mistakes, using your own canon within the canon while claiming to value each verse equally, all of that is not loving the Bible, it's loving your own reading or interpretation of the Bible."

— BRIAN QUINCY NEWCOMB

New Covenant Theology was the "new thing" a few decades ago and many were called heretics for defending and promoting it.

Previously, the two main theologies were Covenant Theology and Dispensationalism.

According to Wikipedia:

"New Covenant Theology (teaches) that the person and work of Jesus Christ is the central focus of the Bible. One distinctive result of this is that Old Testament Laws have been abrogated or cancelled with Jesus' crucifixion, and replaced with the Law of Christ found in the New Covenant."

This view also says that:

"The New Testament interpret(s) the Old Testament...when the NT interprets an OT promise differently than the plain reading, then New Covenant Theology concludes that that is how God interprets His promise."

"As an example, Amos 9:11-12 is quoted by James in Acts 15 and is interpreted by him to associate the rebuilding of "David's fallen tent" with the Gentiles' salvation. This would be a highly surprising interpretation to the Jewish believers, since there is no precedent for it to be interpreted as anything other than a promise to the nation of Israel. (Instead), New Covenant Theology says that God has given us His interpretation of that passage, through James."

WHERE NCT FALTERS IS IN FULLY ADMITTING THAT THE REVELATION OF THE FATHER FOUND IN JESUS IS OFTEN AT ODDS WITH WHAT THE OLD COVENANT PROPHETS HAVE TO SAY ABOUT HIM.

As for me, New Covenant Theology has been my own personal perspective on scripture for a while now. Most of what I have written over the last few years has been from this perspective.

But lately, my theology has started to progress a bit further than this.

I embraced New Covenant Theology because it affirmed that the Flat Bible perspective is flawed and reorients scripture with Christ as our ultimate authority. But unfortunately it stops short of allowing Jesus to fully reform our ideas about God.

So, while New Covenant Theology (NCT) affirms Christ as the center of scripture, it fails to completely embrace Jesus as our one and only image of who the Father is and what He is really like.

Where NCT falters is in fully admitting that the revelation of the Father found in Jesus is often at odds with what the Old Covenant prophets have to say about Him.

Furthermore, the NCT position also fails to admit that the prophets themselves are often at odds with one another about what God said and what God's character was like (as we have previously seen in the differing scriptures about whether God did, or did not, command the Israelites to offer animal sacrifices).

To help explain this, let me borrow an analogy. There are various answers to the question "Where do babies come from?" and someone might say "the stork brings them" and another might say "when mommy and daddy love each other very much the baby starts to grow in her tummy" and still another might say "the male contributes the sperm which he secretes during sexual intercourse to fertilize the egg which the woman provides and in 9 months the embryo matures into a fetus and a child is born."

Two of those answers might be considered "true", one of them is obviously a story designed to symbolize the reality without actually addressing any of the mechanics, and yet all of them are still an attempt to answer the question about where babies come from.

This is similar to what we have in the Hebrew Bible when it comes to the question of what God is like. Some voices give us the "stork" version of the story, with great symbolism and hyperbole. Some voices give us an approximation of the answer. Other voices may give us more detailed and specific answers that more closely align with reality.

For us, Jesus is the reality. He is "the exact representation" of the Father. He is the one in whom "the fullness of the Deity lives in bodily form." He is "the Word made flesh who dwelt among us."

So, the best picture of the Father is found in Christ. If we have "seen Him," we have truly and accurately "seen the Father" in the most complete and full way possible. Why? Because "no one has ever seen God" except Jesus, and the reason He came was to reveal the Father to us like no one else before ever did, or could.

In our analogy, David the Psalmist might be one who provides the more poetic "stork version" of the Father's character. Isaiah and Jeremiah might be the "mommy loves daddy" version of the story. But only Christ gives us the version of the story that includes every specific detail we need to fully understand who the Father is and what the Father is like.

As long as we insist upon holding tightly to the rigid inerrancy of the Old Testament scriptures, we will forever be kept from fully embracing the clearest and most accurate portrayal of who God really is.

Until we relax our grip on the idea that the Old Testament prophets were truly seeing God clearly and recognize that the Abba Father we see revealed in Christ overrides those limited and flawed perspectives of God, we will remain confused about who God really is.

As long as we allow the tarnished testimony of Moses to describe God as one who commands His people to slaughter infants and toddlers without showing compassion, we will forever stand in opposition to the testimony of Jesus who showed us an Abba Father God who loves children, cares for His enemies, shows compassion to the broken and commands us to do the same - specifically because this is who He is and what He is like. (See Matt. 5:44-45)

So, even as those who stood up and defended the New Covenant Theology view a few decades ago were considered heretics and false teachers by the Dispensationalists and Covenant Theology teachers of their day, we should not be surprised when the same charge is leveled at those of us who affirm a Jesus-centric perspective of God today.

Ultimately I believe it simply boils down to this: Who is our authority? Is it the Bible? Or is it Christ? Do we center our theology on a book, or on a person who is indeed God Himself incarnate?

The Book, as wonderful as it may be, is imperfect. It contains the testimony of men who sometimes saw clearly and sometimes did not. The Book contains the voices of men who don't always agree with one another about who God is and what God is like.

Our choice is simple: We either agree with Jesus about who God is, because He is God made flesh, or we side with those Old Testament prophets who were not perfect, not flawless and not "God with us" in the flesh. The choice should be easy.

GOD-BREATHED?

In the ongoing debate about whether or not the Word of God is Jesus, or simply a Book about Jesus, the argument is always raised that "All scripture is God-breathed" (2 Timothy 3:16) and therefore no one has any authority to question the Bible.

There are more than a few problems with this. First of all, when Paul wrote those words, he was not thinking of the "Bible" in the same way that you and I might think of it today.

To Paul, and to most First Century believers, the "Scriptures" were the Law and the Prophets and the Books of Wisdom, which would include the Psalms. It probably also included works that most Protestants today do not consider to be scripture like the Book of Enoch (which gets quoted in the New Testament book of Jude) and the Wisdom of Solomon and other Hebrew writings like Sirach and Tobit, that many considered to be Holy writings.

One thing for certain is that Paul was not thinking of his own epistles when he said this. It must be stressed that Paul did not think that he was writing Scripture when he wrote to the churches in Ephesus, Corinth, Rome, etc. He was writing letters to various Christian communities who needed encouragement and wisdom about certain challenges that threatened their faith.

He also was most certainly not thinking about any of the four Gospels which were not even written when he said this.

Yes, we are very blessed to have copies of some of those epistles, and other Apostolic writings, but none of those people had any inkling that they were writing something that one day might be added to a book alongside Genesis, Isaiah or Malachi and considered scripture.

Secondly, the book that eventually became known as the Bible went through several wildly different forms before finally being Canonized in the Fourth Century. Before this the church referred to a fluid collection of Hebrew scriptures and First Century Apostolic writings and the various Gospel accounts for insight.

As New Testament scholar David Bentley Hart says in the introduction to his most recent translation of the New Testament:

> "*There is no single definitive text of the New Testament canon.* Among the oldest manuscripts we have, no text in the New Testament, nor any complete collection of the New Testament texts, wholly agrees with every other version…this presents a problem for the literalist believer in 'verbal inspiration'; *for if, indeed an absolutely pure text of scripture somewhere exists, we have no notion whatsoever where it is to be found…*during the first several centuries of the church, it was widely known that there was a great variety of differing versions of biblical texts, and this seemed to perturb no one very much. In fact, it was many centuries before what we regard as the New Testament canon gained universal acceptance; *in many places, books we do not now tend to regard as canonical were treated as sacred scripture, while other books that we assume to be part of Christian scripture*

were either unknown or rejected as dubious." (David Bentley Hart, "The New Testament", page xxxiii)

In other words, the early Christian's idea of "scripture" looked radically different from ours and, depending on who you were talking to and what time in Church history, you might be surprised what was considered scripture and what was not.

For example, several New Testament books that every Protestant today considers an essential part of the Bible were, at various times and by various Church Fathers, eliminated from the accepted Canon of Scripture. Books like, Hebrews, Jude, Revelation, 2 Peter, 2 and 3 John and James were left out of several lists of accepted books of scripture by many church leaders.

Consequently, many other books that most Protestants have never even heard of were accepted by some as Canon like the Didache, the Shepherd of Hermas, the Book of Baruch, Jubilees and the Letter of Jeremiah, for example.

> THE EARLY CHRISTIAN'S IDEA OF "SCRIPTURE" LOOKED RADICALLY DIFFERENT FROM OURS AND, DEPENDING ON WHO YOU WERE TALKING TO AND WHAT TIME IN CHURCH HISTORY, YOU MIGHT BE SURPRISED WHAT WAS CONSIDERED SCRIPTURE AND WHAT WAS NOT.

Sometime around 363 AD several attempts were made to establish an official and accepted list of which books or epistles were scripture and which should be eliminated. There was no firm consensus on the contents of that list for several decades, but eventually a group of Christian leaders—whose names the average Christian does not even know—decided for the rest of us forevermore which books were to be accepted and which were to be rejected as scripture.

Today there is still no universal consensus on what is and what is not the "Bible" or Holy Scripture.

Like the early church, depending on who you ask, and where you live, and what Christian tradition you belong to, the book you carry around and refer to as the Holy Bible might look very different from another book from another Christian community that might be called the "Bible."

I've started to wonder, "How do we know those people who decided what was and what wasn't Scripture got it right?" Furthermore, I've started to wonder who gave those men the authority to decide that God was no longer speaking to His people and inspiring them to write down what the Holy Spirit was revealing to them about the nature and character of God?

Why do we so blindly accept the authority of these name-less and faceless men who made these decisions for the rest of us? What if they didn't really have the authority to make this decision? What if they left writings out, or included writings, in error? How are we so sure that they were inerrant and infallible in their process?

Ultimately, for those who insist on inerrancy and infallibility of scripture, what they are actually trusting in is the "perfection" of those decisions made by a group of people centuries ago about what was and wasn't worthy to be included in the Bible.

One friend of mine told me that, in his opinion, the Bible we have today is exactly what God wanted us to have and that He made sure we received the true inspired scriptures that we use today. But, if this is so, then I have a few questions, like: Why did God wait nearly 400 years to give the Church these inspired scriptures? And, why did God give the Western Christian Church only 66 books, but decided to give the Roman Catholics 73 books and the Ethiopan Orthodox Christians received 81 books in their Canon?

The problem, of course, is that we have such a narrow view of God's sovereign plan. When it comes to our faith tradition, God must have been in complete control. But in the case of those other Christian traditions, God must have decided not to guide anything as carefully as He did with ours.

This places us in the conveniently favored position and everyone else in the left-over category. Does God really work this way? Or is it possible that, in every case, different people made different choices about which books to include and which to exclude based on a set of criteria that had very little to do with the perfect will of God and much more to do with the views of Christian leaders in that particular faith community.

Ultimately, it boils down to this: Our scriptures are a loose collection of writings by various people throughout history who were inspired by God to write down what they believed was true about Him, and to testify about what they experienced of God.

Some of what we may currently accept as scripture might not actually be inspired by the Holy Spirit. Some of the scriptures that we reject, or are simply unaware of, might actually be worth considering as a legitimate source of wisdom about God. But everything—and I do mean everything—needs to be filtered through the lens of Christ. If it lines up with our revelation of Him, we should take it to heart. If it disagrees with the Word of God who became flesh and came to dwell within us, we should dismiss it as being the flawed testimony of men.

We must also keep in mind that while the official Canon of Scripture may be closed, this does not mean that God stopped speaking to His people in 400 AD. God is always at work, He is always speaking, and His people have been filled by the Holy Spirit and inspired to write books, and poems, and songs, and to paint and compose and to express the marvelous wonders of Christ for thousands of years now. From John Chrysostom and St. John of the Cross, to A.W. Tozer and Max Lucado. Not all of it is true, and none of it should necessarily be considered "scripture," but there is much that we may find is very inspired and worthy of our consideration.

How do we discern what is true or not? Jesus is our hermeneutic. Jesus is our ultimate authority. Everything we read is subject to Him. If it speaks of Christ, points to Christ, glorifies Christ or agrees with Christ, we should take it to heart. Of course, we should never allow anything to supersede Christ's authority in our lives. But all truth is His Truth.

So, before you claim that the Bible is the infallible and inerrant Word of God because Paul claimed that "all scripture is God-breathed" be sure to remember that what he considered scripture and what you're currently referring to as scripture are not necessarily the same.

Also, remember that just because something is "God-breathed" doesn't mean it is infallible and inerrant. Humans are also "God-breathed" and we are neither infallible or inerrant.

Yes, scripture, whatever that might be, "is inspired by God and profitable for teaching, for reproof, for correction, for training in righteousness" but determining how and in what ways scripture is profitable for us is something that must be discerned by the Holy Spirit of God that lives within each and every one of us.

This should cause each of us to cling more to Jesus and to dive deeper into Christ for wisdom and insight.

After all, if we abide in Him then we experience Christ abiding in us, and this is the only way any of us can bear fruit.

"MY OWN POSITION IS NOT FUNDAMENTALIST IF FUNDAMENTALISM MEANS ACCEPTING AS A POINT OF FAITH AT THE OUTSET THE PROPOSITION 'EVERY STATEMENT IN THE BIBLE IS COMPLETELY TRUE IN THE LITERAL, HISTORICAL SENSE'. THAT WOULD BREAK DOWN AT ONCE ON THE PARABLES.

ALL THE SAME COMMON SENSE AND GENERAL UNDERSTANDING OF LITERARY KINDS WHICH WOULD FORBID ANYONE TO TAKE THE PARABLES AS HISTORICAL STATEMENTS, CARRIED A VERY LITTLE FURTHER, WOULD FORCE US TO DISTINGUISH BETWEEN:

- BOOKS LIKE ACTS OR THE ACCOUNT OF DAVID'S REIGN, WHICH ARE EVERYWHERE DOVETAILED INTO A KNOWN HISTORY, GEOGRAPHY, AND GENEALOGIES,

- BOOKS LIKE ESTHER, OR JONAH OR JOB WHICH DEAL WITH OTHERWISE UNKNOWN CHARACTERS LIVING IN UNSPECIFIED PERIODS, AND PRETTY WELL PROCLAIM THEMSELVES TO BE SACRED FICTION.

SUCH DISTINCTIONS ARE NOT NEW. CALVIN LEFT THE HISTORICITY OF JOB AN OPEN QUESTION AND FROM EARLIER, ST. JEROME SAID THAT THE WHOLE MOSAIC ACCOUNT OF CREATION WAS DONE 'AFTEJUS, (OR, "AFTER THE FACT").

OF COURSE, I BELIEVE THE COMPOSITION, PRESENTATION, AND SELECTION FOR INCLUSION IN THE BIBLE, OF ALL BOOKS TO HAVE BEEN GUIDED BY THE HOLY GHOST. BUT I THINK HE MEANT US TO HAVE SACRED MYTH AND SACRED FICTION AS WELL AS SACRED HISTORY."

—CS LEWIS[1]

CHAPTER 9

WHO SAID THAT?

"Saul (of Tarsus) was a Biblical literalist who weaponized Scriptures to justify killing Christians. Saul worshiped the book. Paul worshipped the Christ."

— RICHARD MURRAY

Jesus is famous for his list of blessings found in the Sermon on the Mount. You know, "Blessed are the poor for they will inherit the earth" and "Blessed are the peacemakers for they shall be called the children of God."

But the Old Testament also contains a few "blessed are" statements which don't always sound quite as beautiful.

For example, can you imagine Jesus saying something like this:

"Blessed is the one who seizes your infants and dashes them on the rocks." (Ps 137:8-9)

That's not the sort of thing we would ever expect Jesus to say, is it? This is partly why we need to learn how to read the Old Testament scriptures through the lens of Jesus.

See, before we can understand a text, we first need to understand God—and that means recognizing Him for who He really
is.

The best way to understand God is to look at Jesus. Why?
Because, as we have seen over and over again, Jesus is the one
who reveals the Father to us.

So, when we read a verse of scripture in the Hebrew Bible
that has God saying something like:

> "Samaria will be held guilty, for she has rebelled against her
> God. They will fall by the sword, their little ones will be dashed
> in pieces, and their pregnant women will be ripped open."
> (Hosea 13:16)

ULTIMATELY WE HAVE TO DECIDE IF OUR FAITH IS IN A BOOK, OR IF OUR FAITH IS IN JESUS.

We need to ask ourselves a few questions first, like: "Is this what God said?" or, "Is this what the author thought God was saying?"

Actually, our first question should be: "Does this sound like
something Jesus would ever say?"

If not, we know that the verse we're reading isn't what God
said but what the author thought God was saying. Because ultimately we have to decide if our faith is in a Book, or if our faith
is in Jesus.

In this specific case, we can see that Jesus showed great love
and compassion for people from Samaria. He told parables where
the Samaritans were the heroes. He went out of his way to share
the Gospel with a Samaritan woman. He refused to look down
on Samaritans or to treat them any differently than other people.

Jesus loved Samaritans. So, we can be very sure of one thing:
Jesus would not encourage anyone to "dash in pieces" their "little ones" or to "rip open" their "pregnant women."

Not even a little bit.

There are over 100 verses in the Bible where God reportedly told people to go and kill other people. In many of those verses God seems to command people to slaughter women, children and even toddlers and pregnant mothers.

If you think Jesus would ever do this you might want to refresh your memory a little. He is the same one who told us to love our enemies, bless those who curse us, forgive those who hate us, pray for those who misuse us and overcome evil with good.

In fact, Jesus tells us to do all of these things so that we can be like someone else: His Father in Heaven.

Yes, our compassion, forgiveness and radical love is patterned after the same love that God has for everyone—both the righteous and the unrighteous.

> "But I say to you, love your enemies and pray for those who persecute you, so that you may be sons of your Father who is in heaven; for He causes His sun to rise on the evil and the good, and sends rain on the righteous and the unrighteous." (Matt. 5:44-45)

If God wasn't kind and merciful to everyone, then Jesus would have no basis for asking us to be like Him by showing love and mercy for our enemies.

Jesus reveals a God who would rather die for His enemies than kill them. Jesus shows us a God who loves all the people we hate and He wants us to love them, too.

So, the next time you read a verse in the Bible that depicts God as a bloodthirsty warrior who delights at the slaughter of women, children and pregnant mothers, just remember: That's not Jesus. And if it doesn't look like Jesus, it's not the Father.

For too long many of us have embraced a religion that is based on believing certain doctrines and defending traditions of our faith. This comes mostly from what we have heard from others—our parents, our family, our church—about who God is and what God is like. It defines Christianity, and the Christian life, as nothing more than believing what the Bible says, or what our denomination or church tells us it says.

But the time is ripe for us to shed this dead religion in favor of a more vibrant and living relationship with a person—not a book or a creed or a statement of faith—but a God "in whom we live and move and have our being." (See Acts 17:28)

This is a living faith. In contrast to an inherited religion, a living faith is about an actual relationship with the person that the Bible points to. It's about knowing God and His Son in an intimate way.

All through the Gospels Jesus urges us to abandon the perceived safety of religious information-gathering to the truly abundant life found only by abiding in Him.

For example:

- We are called into an intimacy with God that is scandalous and breath-taking. (Matt. 6:9)

- He is our "Papa" and we are His children. (1 John 3:1)

- He invites us to draw near. (James 4:8)

- He wants to make His home in us. (John 14:23)

- He wants us to experience an intimacy with Him that compares to the union of a husband and wife. (Eph. 5:32)

- He wants us to experience a "knowing" of Himself that conceives something within us. (John 17:3)

- What this intimacy conceives in us is a new life that comes only from our close connection with Himself. (2 Cor. 5:17; Rev. 21:5)

The sad thing is, too many of those who profess themselves to be Christians are not experiencing Christ in this way. They have not yet moved from secondhand religion into a firsthand knowledge of God where His voice is heard, His mind is known, and their heartbeats are in sync with His own.

Religion leads to a life of anxiety, fear and stress. A living faith in Christ leads to a life of joy, hope, peace and confidence based on our connection to God.

If you're still stuck in religion, I invite you to begin moving into a firsthand experience of God through the Spirit of Christ.

It can be as simple as taking some time to sit quietly alone with the Lord and whispering a prayer to Him, asking for a deeper experience of His presence; being still to know that He is God.

It won't happen all at once, but if you are serious about abandoning your secondhand religion in order to enter into firsthand knowledge of God, you will be rewarded.

> "…they should seek God, in the hope that they might feel after Him and find Him, although He is not far from each one of us." (Acts 17:27)

> "Blessed are those who hunger and thirst after God, for they shall be filled…Blessed are the pure in heart, for they shall see God." (Matt. 5:6;8)

> "…and they shall call him 'Immanuel', which means 'God with us'" (Matt. 1:23)

Are you ready to move from mere religion to an experiential faith in Christ? He is closer than your own heartbeat and longing to show you more of Himself.

CHAPTER 10

THE LITERAL HERESY

"[The biblical] stories of violence mirror how ancient tribal cultures saw the gods. The flood, massacre of Canaanites, and other such acts of violence don't tell us what God is like but how the Israelites, an ancient tribal people, understood and worshiped God...the Bible is not a handy information packet on God from A-Z but a record of Israel's understanding of God, often penetrating and consoling, but also incomplete and disturbing."

— PETER ENNS, *THE SIN OF CERTAINTY*

The first real "heretic" of Christianity was a man named "Marcion" who saw the radical difference between the God of the Old Testament scriptures and the God revealed by Jesus. But this was not his heresy. In fact, many—if not all—early Christians also saw this same radical difference between the two testimonies of God's nature.

What's more, all of those early Christians also rejected the violence of God in the Old Testament scriptures and fully embraced the radical enemy-love taught by Jesus. There are no dissenting voices in the early Christian church when it comes to non-violence and enemy love whatsoever. They all saw Jesus as a non-violent Messiah who taught His disciples to love their enemies and turn the other cheek, even if it got them all killed. (But this is another issue).

So, what was Marcion's heresy? It was his solution for responding to the differing perspectives of God between those two Testaments that got him labeled a heretic. Marcion's response was to literally throw out the entire Old Covenant and to claim that the God revealed in those Hebrew scriptures was actually a demon. Now, that's a heresy!

THE MOST SURPRISING THING ABOUT ORIGEN'S REBUKE OF MARCION WAS THAT HE REALIZED THAT THE HERESY WAS ROOTED IN ONE THING: READING THE BIBLE LITERALLY.

When Origen, another early Christian, wrote to rebuke Marcion's extreme response, it was not to dismiss the idea that there were obvious differences between the way God was viewed in the two Covenants. In fact, Origen agreed with Marcion that there were differences between God as Moses and the other Old Testament prophets spoke of Him and the "Abba" Father God as revealed through Jesus.

The most surprising thing about Origen's rebuke of Marcion was that he realized that the heresy was rooted in one thing: Reading the Bible literally.

The reason that is so surprising—even ironic—is that there are Christians today who insist on reading the Bible literally and yet still consider Marcion a heretic.

In other words, today's Bible Literalists see Marcionism as a heresy even though the sin of Marcionism is specifically defined by Origen as reading the Bible too literally.

What they miss is that no one considered Marcionism a heresy for claiming that Jesus was right about who God was and what God looked like. Every early Christian embraced that idea. All of them.

The idea that Jesus was—and is—the clearest picture anyone could ever have of God was universally accepted by the early Christian Church.

This was not heresy. It was Christianity.

Origen agreed with Marcion that a literal view of God as seen in the Old Testament scriptures *"would not be entertained regarding the most unjust and cruel of men"* and went on to say:

> "Holy Scripture is not understood by [Marcion] according to its spiritual, but according to its literal meaning" (Origen, *De Principiis*, 4:8-9)

In other words, Marcion went off the rails because he read the Bible too literally. By reading the Bible literally, Marcion could not reconcile the God of Moses—who commanded genocide and delighted in the dashing of infants against the rocks—and the God of Jesus—who showed love and mercy to the just and the unjust and forgave sinners freely.

Therefore, Marcion could only do one thing: He jettisoned the entire Hebrew Bible and rejected the God he read about there as a demonic aberration of Jesus' "Abba" Father God.

But, as Origen and the other Church Fathers demonstrated, there is a better way to respond. Instead of taking everything we read in the Old Testament about God as a literal fact—as if those words are dictated by God and transcribed by dispassionate observers with no bias of their own—we should read those scriptures through the lens of Jesus.

Jesus is our best and most accurate testament of who God really is.

Rejecting Marcionism needs to include a rejection of a literal reading of the Old Testament scriptures.

For that matter, if you and I read the Old Testament scriptures the way Paul the Apostle did, we'd be called heretics.

For example, if you read Psalm 18:40-49, the passage is all about how God will destroy the Gentiles and pour out His vengeance on them:

> "I destroyed my foes. They cried for help, but there was no one to save them— to the Lord, but he did not answer.

> "I beat them as fine as windblown dust; I trampled them like mud in the streets. You have delivered me from the attacks of the people; you have made me the head of nations.

> "People I did not know now serve me, foreigners cower before me; as soon as they hear of me, they obey me. They all lose heart; they come trembling from their strongholds.

> "The Lord lives! Praise be to my Rock! Exalted be God my Savior! He is the God who avenges me, who subdues nations under me, who saves me from my enemies.

> "You exalted me above my foes; from a violent man you rescued me. *Therefore, I will praise you, Lord, among the nations; I will sing the praises of your name.*"

It's pretty gruesome stuff, to be honest. But notice how Paul the Apostle quotes—or rather heavily *misquotes* – this exact same text in Romans 15:9:

> "For I tell you that Christ has become a servant of the Jews on behalf of God's truth, to confirm the promises made to the patriarchs so that the Gentiles may glorify God for His mercy, as it is written:

> "*...Therefore I will praise you, Lord, among the nations; I will sing the praises of your name.*"

This is what you call "taking scripture out of context" my friends.

Paul completely takes a passage about how God will take vengeance on the Gentiles and destroy them and misquotes it as a way to prove that God is actually glorified for showing *mercy* to the Gentiles.

Trust me: No Christian pastor or Bible teacher would ever get away with anything so irresponsible as this today. And this is not the only example. Oh, no.

Paul does it again in the very next verse of Romans 15:10 when he radically misquotes Deuteronomy 32:43 which says:

> "Again it says, 'Rejoice O Gentiles, with His people, for He will avenge the blood of His servants, He will take vengeance on His enemies, and make atonement for His land and people."

But Paul quotes this verse and leaves out all the violent passages, opting instead to only mention this part:

> "Again it says, 'Rejoice O Gentiles, with His people…'"

What's going on here? How can Paul do such a thing? Is he trying to pull a fast one? Hardly. Instead, Paul is reading the Old Testament scriptures through the lens of Christ. He starts by knowing who God is—who He really is—by looking at Jesus.

New Testament scholar, David Bentley Hart, affirms Paul's allegorical approach and makes note of how his practice impacted the way later Christian teachers interpreted the Old Testament scriptures:

> "As should be obvious, Paul frequently allegorizes Hebrew scripture; the 'spiritual reading' of scripture typical of the Church Fathers of the early centuries was not their invention, nor just something borrowed from pagan culture, but was already a widely accepted hermeneutical practice among Jewish scholars. So it is not anachronistic to read Paul here as saying that the stories he is repeating are not accurate historical accounts of actual events, but allegorical tales composed for the edification of readers."[1]

By reading the scriptures through the lens of Christ, Paul can clearly see that the Father is NOT a God of vengeance and wrath.

He understands that Jesus has subverted that Old Covenant idea of God and revealed to us a God who shows mercy, loves everyone, and redeems even His enemies.

See, there was a time when Paul went by the name "Saul of Tarsus" and he went around doing what any good Pharisee did—he persecuted anyone who dared to question the authority of Scripture.

In fact, it was in the act of persecuting the Christian church that Jesus showed up, knocked him off his ass (literally) and opened Paul's eyes to the truth: God wasn't pleased with violence.

Paul experienced mercy and forgiveness from the very people he was trying to murder. He heard the Gospel of Peace for the first time and very soon he came to realize that God was not who he thought He was.

After this, Paul counted all of that scriptural "expertise" as manure and devoted himself to one thing: "to know Christ and the power of His resurrection" (Phil. 3:10)

Why would Paul do that? Why is it so important to "know Christ"?

Because without Christ, you and I cannot see God. There is a veil that covers our eyes if we try to understand the Scriptures without reading them through the lens of Jesus. (See 2 Cor. 3:15)

This is why Paul could now read violent passages in the Hebrew Scriptures and dismiss them as the flawed perspectives of men who had yet to know Christ as he had now come to know Him.

By knowing Christ, Paul could now clearly see who the "Abba" Father God really was: A God who looked and acted like Jesus.

As long as we continue to follow the letter of the Law, we will reap death. (Romans 7:10)

Paul and the other Apostles invite us to see God through brand new eyes: The eyes of Jesus. Through Him, we can clearly see a God who refuses to beat His children. Instead, we see an Abba who longs to draw everyone to Himself and transform each of us into people who look and act like Jesus.

The bottom line is that we will never know God apart from Jesus. We will never discover the path to peace apart from following the Prince of Peace.

> "No one who denies the Son has the Father; whoever acknowledges the Son has the Father also." (1 John 2:23)

Jesus is the "Word of God" and the "Word of God" is Jesus.

What many of us need to understand is that the Old Testament scriptures are filled with "Pre-Christian" ideas.

This comes as a very real shock to many of us, but if we take time to think about it, we'll see that it's true.

Yes, the Old Testament scriptures prophesied that the Messiah would come, and they told us about what He would do, and what His Kingdom would look like, and much more. But those scriptures are Pre-Christian. They foretell the Messiah's coming, but they do not contain Him.

For many, the Bible has become the veil that covers the face of Moses, or the demand for a mediator who would report God's words back to us so we don't have to face Him ourselves.

WHAT MANY OF US NEED TO UNDERSTAND IS THAT THE OLD TESTAMENT SCRIPTURES ARE FILLED WITH "PRE-CHRISTIAN" IDEAS.

God's heart has always been to have a one-on-one relationship with each of us. We keep trying to put leaders and kings and prophets and priests and pastors and scriptures between us and Him.

We often want a representative, but not God Himself. We want a rule book to follow, not a relationship with a living God.

We want a pattern to follow, but God wants a conversation.

The danger of rules and patterns is that we can fall into the rhythms they create and function without any need for God at all. And this is why God continually tears down those formulaic, man-made barriers that keep us from Him—and Him from us.

The heart of the New Covenant is simply this: *"I will be their God, and they will be my people."*

We seem to always drift towards religion, but God is constantly calling us into a living, breathing life where we can interact with Him.

Please, don't hide your God in a book. Don't bind Jesus in genuine leather when He has come to live and breathe inside of you.

CHAPTER 11

INFALLIBLE, INERRANT, OR INCARNATE?

"The Word of God is infallible, inerrant and totally inspired. And when He was about 18, He grew a beard."

— BRAD JERSAK

For those who embrace—even insist—on the inerrancy and infallibility of the Bible, there emerges a very odd version of a God who simply cannot make up His mind about things.

As an example, the infallible Scriptures are 100 percent clear about the fact that God causes evil and creates disasters:

"When disaster [literally "evil"] comes to a city, has not the Lord caused it?" (Amos 3:6)

"I form the light and create darkness, I bring prosperity and create disaster ["evil"]; I the Lord, do all these things." (Isaiah 45:7)

"The LORD said to him, "Who gave human beings their mouths? Who makes them deaf or mute? Who gives them sight or makes them blind? Is it not I, the LORD?" (Exodus 4:11)

These verses, and several others like them, affirm without any doubt that God is the one who brings disaster, creates evil and makes people deaf and blind.

This is an inerrant and infallible statement of fact supported by an equally infallible and inerrant Holy Bible.

However, there are other scriptures that contradict these ideas and instead say:

"God is light, and in Him there is no darkness at all" (1 John 1:5)

"His works are perfect, and all his ways are just. A faithful God who does no wrong, upright and just is he" (Deut. 32:4)

Jesus also affirmed that it was Satan who came to "steal, kill and destroy," not God. So, taking all of these infallible and inerrant verses together, we know without a doubt that God does no wrong, and doesn't destroy or kill, but that He most certainly brings evil, creates darkness and hands out birth defects.

We also know that God was the one who commanded David to take a census and then punished 70,000 people by killing them with a plague when David obeyed. (See 2 Sam. 24:1)

At the same time, we clearly see that it was Satan who incited David to take a census, not God. (See 1 Chronicles 21:1)

We also know that God never tempts anyone to do evil. (See James 1:13)

So clearly these inerrant and infallible verses tell us that God, and Satan, both commanded David to take a census and then God punished David and his people for giving in to the temptation which God never tempted him with.

Does that make sense to you?

Try this one:

"Just as it pleased the Lord to make you prosper and increase in number, so it will please Him to ruin and destroy you." (Deut. 28:63)

"As surely as I live, declares the Sovereign Lord, I take no pleasure in the death of the wicked!" (Ezekiel 33:11)

So, God is pleased to destroy His people, but He takes no pleasure in their death.

One more:

"I, the Lord your God, am a jealous God, punishing the children for the sins of the fathers." (Exodus 20:5; Deut. 5:9)

"As surely as I live, declares the Sovereign Lord, you will no longer quote this proverb in Israel...he will not die for his father's sin; he will surely live, but his father will die for his own sin... the son will not share the guilt of the father, nor will the father share the guilt of the son." (Ezekiel 18:3;17-19)

Clearly, according to these inerrant and infallible verses of scripture, God punishes children for the sins of their fathers, but a son will not die for his father's sins, nor share the guilt of his father, nor will the father share the guilt of his son.

Got it? If you do, please explain it to the rest of us.

All I can see is that there are competing voices in the scriptures. Some prophets see God one way—*causing evil, creating birth defects and punishing sons for the sins of their fathers*—and other prophets see God a different way—*not causing evil or tempting people, or punishing sons for their father's sins and taking no pleasure in the death of anyone.*

THOSE WHO INSIST ON AN INERRANT SCRIPTURE IGNORE THESE DISCREPANCIES, OR TURN SOMERSAULTS TO MAKE EACH CONTRADICTORY STATEMENT TRUE WHILE IGNORING THE VERY OBVIOUS FACT: *THE VOICES WE HEAR IN SCRIPTURE ARE NOT INFALLIBLE, NOR INERRANT.*

Those who insist on an inerrant scripture ignore these discrepancies, or turn somersaults to make each contradictory statement true while ignoring the very obvious fact: *The voices we hear in scripture are not infallible, nor inerrant.*

So, what can we do about these verses? How can we discern which ones speak truthfully about God's character and which verses miss the mark?

According to Paul, *"The person with the Spirit makes judgments about all things"* (1 Cor. 2:15) and while quoting Isaiah's rhetorical question *"Who has known the mind of the Lord so as to instruct Him!?"* (Isa. 4:13) responds shockingly: *"But we have the mind of Christ!"* (v. 17)

So, who dares to challenge and question the scriptures? We do! Why? Because we have the mind of Christ.

Paul even reminds us that we will judge angels (1 Cor. 6:3); and who are "angels" but "messengers from God"? (The word "angel" in scripture is literally translated as "messenger of God")

Do we have an obligation to read the Scriptures through the lens of Jesus and with the mind of Christ? Absolutely!

Otherwise we are left with a schizophrenic God who is both good and evil, who is both tempting and never-tempting, who both creates birth defects and heals them, who delights in destruction and takes no pleasure in it, etc.

Is God the author of confusion? No.

Is God the one who is confused about who He is and what He does, or could it be that those who wrote about Him prior to Christ couldn't see Him as clearly as we do now?

If you have seen Jesus, you have seen the Father. There is no clearer picture of Him than this.

The only way to know God any better is to know Jesus. The more you come to know Him, the more you can clearly see through the mind of Christ what God is like.

Another thing to consider as we look at the inerrancy or infallibility of scripture is how many different versions of the scriptures there are, and how much of what we consider to be "the Word of God" in our English Bibles is actually an embellishment of earlier texts.

For example, before the New Testament was written, the Bible used by most people in the first century was a Greek translation of the Hebrew Scriptures called the Septuagint. Essentially, it was the Old Testament Bible used by the New Testament authors. But what most Christians don't realize is that the Septuagint sometimes reveals an older version of the Hebrew Scriptures than the versions we currently use in our seminaries and universities, or that appear in our English Bibles. Therefore, the Septuagint gives us a glimpse into the earlier stages of the Bible's development—and access to Hebrew Scriptures that are older than the texts that form the basis of our modern translations.

As one Biblical scholar notes:

> "This is especially problematic for those who put their entire faith in the pursuit of the 'original text.'" (Timothy M. Law)

Why does he say this? Because, the older versions of the Hebrew texts found in the Septuagint reveal some startling facts about our own Old Testament scriptures. For example:

> "One of the best-known stories from the Old Testament is that of David and Goliath. In the Septuagint, the story is about half the length as the account in the Hebrew Bible. It lacks the details about David delivering food to his brothers, his first hearing of Goliath's challenge, and his contemplation on the risk/reward of getting involved (17:12-31). Also missing are the covenant Jonathan makes with David (18:1-5) and the story of Saul's evil spirit (18:10-11).

> "Careful study reveals that the Septuagint version is definitely the earlier form of the story–*the Septuagint didn't just "leave things out" by mistake. It was translated from an earlier version of the Hebrew Bible where these details were absent.* The version of the story we know is a later, expanded, version."[1]

So, in other words, many of the details about the life of David that we consider to be part of the Biblical Canon—inerrant and infallible and unquestionably the "Word of God"—were added in much later by people other than the original writers of the text. This begs the question then for Biblicists: If the Bible is inspired, inerrant and infallible, are we to assume that whomever added in those details about David's life, years later, was also inspired by God?

Keep in mind that the Apostles who wrote our New Testament used the Septuagint and considered it to be inspired by God. So, do we agree with the Apostles about what scriptures were inspired, or do we agree with later Church leaders who Canonized the Bible we have today?

DO WE AGREE WITH THE APOSTLES ABOUT WHAT SCRIPTURES WERE INSPIRED, OR DO WE AGREE WITH LATER CHURCH LEADERS WHO CANONIZED THE BIBLE WE HAVE TODAY

Hopefully this realization about the origins of our Scriptures doesn't shake your faith. If so, I apologize because this is not my intention. However, questions like this can help us to discover who, or what, our faith is really in: Is it in a Book, or is it in a God who has revealed Himself to us by His Spirit?

Unfortunately, I have seen many of my friends over the years walk away from their faith in Christ over a shocking revelation about Church hierarchy, or about the various pagan influences within Christianity, or about the falsehood of other doctrines they have held dear.

As sad as this is, I must stress something: If your faith is in your Church, then hard truths about the Church will expose your misplaced faith. If your faith is in a doctrine, then revelations about the falsehood of that doctrine may cause you to walk away from God completely.

But, if your faith is in Christ alone, then nothing is going to change your mind about Him. He is faithful and true. He is closer than a brother. He is alive within you by His Spirit right now and nothing—nothing at all—can ever change that.

Again, my goal here is not to cause anyone to toss out their Bible or abandon their faith in the Scriptures. But, what I do hope to do is to point out that our Bibles are not worthy of our worship. Our Bible points us to Christ, and He is the author and finisher of our faith.

So, what about the Gospels? Are they reliable? Can we trust their accuracy? Let's answer that in the next chapter.

CHAPTER 12

ARE THE GOSPELS RELIABLE?

"The writer of Hebrews said that all before Christ was a mere shadow of the reality (Heb. 10:1). It's kind of hard to decipher the true form of something by looking at its shadow... God is Christ-like, and in him there is no un-Christ-likeness at all. This and this alone can change our hearts of stone back into beating, throbbing hearts of love that manifest the image of the divine."

— JACOB M. WRIGHT

Both skeptical and conservative Christian scholars agree that the four Gospels were not written in Palestine or Israel. This is not in much dispute. But what is in dispute is whether or not those authors—living decades after the life of Christ and in different countries—could have invented the details of the Gospel story, or if they were writing down an oral tradition that had preserved the details accurately.

If the Gospel authors invented these stories and wrote down legends that were not based in reality, then we might expect them to get many details wrong. Since they themselves were not from Palestine or Jerusalem, and since they did not actually experience the Jesus first-hand, they must either have written down the testimonies of others who actually did walk with Jesus, or they wrote down stories that they or others had made up.

In short: The Gospels are either fact or fiction. But how can we know for sure which?

While some skeptics openly doubt whether or not Jesus existed, most of them do not, simply due to the overwhelming evidence. Even the most vocal skeptics, like former Christian professor Bart Ehrman have had to admit that Jesus of Nazareth was an actual historical person, and have even been placed in the unfortunate position of arguing with other skeptics that Jesus was, indeed, an historical figure. "This is not even an issue for scholars of antiquity," says Ehrman. "There is no one who teaches [on this subject] in any University who doubts that Jesus existed. The reason for this is [that] he is abundantly attested in early sources. Early and independent sources indicate that Jesus existed."[1]

This admission is also based on the writings of Paul who casually remarks in his epistles that he knew Mary, the mother of Jesus, and also Peter and James, the brother of Jesus. Therefore, the historicity of Jesus cannot be sincerely doubted based on the abundant evidence. Yes, these skeptics still doubt his miracles, and his divinity, but they cannot dismiss the reality of his historical existence.

If that's not enough, Dr. Robert E. Van Voorst has compiled citations from Roman historians like Thalles, Pliny the Younger, Seutonius, Tacitus, Mara bar Serapion, Lucian of Samosata, and Celus who all affirm the historical Jesus of Nazareth. As he notes:

> "The famous Roman writers on history and imperial affairs have taken pride of place: Suetonius, Tacitus, and Pliny the Younger. On the other end of the spectrum, the comparatively unknown writers Mara and Thallos have also contributed their voices. Philosophic opponents to Christianity such as Lucian and

Celsus have also written about Christ. These writers have a range of opinion: from those perhaps sympathetic to Christ (Mara); through those moderately hostile (Pliny) and those fully hostile but descriptive (Tacitus, Suetonius); to those not interested in description, but who vigorously attack Christianity and in the process attack Christ (Lucian and Celsus). Together, they speak of a variety of topics about Jesus' teachings, movement, and death. And they know that Jesus is worshiped by Christians, which they relate to his founding of a movement"[2]

One thing Dr. Van Voorst points out is that none of these sources—however hostile they may be—ever suggest that Jesus was a fictional character. Finally, he concludes:

"If classical writers had never mentioned Jesus, or especially if they had argued that he was a product of Christian myth-making, then it would be a different matter. They did treat Jesus as a historical person, the founder of his movement, and had no reason to doubt his historicity. It would have been easy (if Jesus never existed) to deliver a strong blow against Christianity by showing that it was based on a myth when it claimed to be based on history. But these writers accepted Jesus as historical, and all but one used the events of his life as arguments against Christianity: he began a movement that they called a pernicious superstition, and he was executed as a criminal."[3]

So, Jesus existed. But what about the Gospels? Are they reliable documents?

One New Testament scholar, Dr. Peter Williams, suggests that one way we can determine the accuracy of those Gospels is to look at the details they report.[4] In other words, if you or I were to write a story about another country we'd never been to that was set 50 or 100 years in the past, we might expect to get more than a few details wrong; like people's names, political events, languages, weather and other cultural specifics.

Try to write a short story that takes place in the Netherlands in 1955, for example. Do you know enough about what was going on in that country at that time in history? Could you guess at the right names for those characters? Would you know what the temperature might be like during the season your story takes place in? Are you aware of who was in power in the Netherlands in 1955?

Of course, you and I could very easily turn to the Internet to quickly answer these sorts of questions. But someone writing in Rome or Syria or Ephesus during the late First or early Second century would have a much harder time determining those sorts of details. We might expect them to make more than a few mistakes regarding the climate, agriculture, current events and economics of the time period—if they were making their stories up.

But if they were writing down stories that had been passed along by eyewitnesses and written down or recorded in some form, then their accuracy about those seemingly insignificant details would be incredibly persuasive.

In other words, how would those people living over fifty years later, and in other countries, ever know those sorts of details any other way?

It would only make sense if they had written down those details that had been given to them by those who really were eyewitnesses to the events. Dr. Williams asserts that those small details point to the authenticity of the Gospels.

Did the Gospel writers give people the right names? After studying about 3,000 names, researchers discovered that Jewish names in Palestine during the early first century occurred at different frequencies than in other areas.

The most common name in the New Testament was Simon. This is true based on the writings of Josephus, the Ossuraries, the Dead Sea Scrolls and the New Testament documents as well.

Joseph is the second most common name found based on those same sources.

What we find is an exact corollary between the top 9 most common male names in both the New Testament documents and other non-scriptural sources of that same time frame.

When researchers looked at the top 9 Jewish names of first century men living in Egypt they got a much different list of names that did not correspond at all to the list of names in Israel.

This means that it's very unlikely that someone living in Egypt, for example, would have been able to guess at the right proportion and types of names to include in a story about Jewish men living in Jerusalem, even if they lived during the same time period. Much less likely that someone living outside of Jerusalem would have been able to accurately guess the types and proportions of Jewish names a half century later.

"It's not just that they have the right proportion of names," says Dr. Williams. "They also have the right features of names."

In other words, we know that there were many Jewish men named Simon living in Israel at the time the Gospels took place. So, if you were to yell the name "Simon!" into a crowd, chances are a lot of men would turn around. That means you'd need to qualify which Simon you meant. This is called "disambiguation". "We find that this is what they did in the New Testament," says Williams. "Jesus had two disciples named 'Simon', one was called 'Cephas' or 'Peter' and the other one was called 'the Zealot' or 'the Canaanite'. Jesus had dinner with a man named 'Simon the Leper'...'Simon of Cyrene' carried the cross for Jesus, etc."

This detail would never have occurred to someone writing in another land who was oblivious to the types and frequency of names in use at that time. They wouldn't have known that Simon was the most common name among Jewish men living in Palestine in the First Century. Therefore, they wouldn't know to call so many people by that name, nor would they know that people needed to add a disambiguation to the name because otherwise it would be confusing as to which Simon was being referred to.

The same thing happens with the most popular female name in the region at that time, Mary. We have Mary the mother of Jesus, Mary the Mother of Joseph, and Mary Magdalene.

The less common names do not receive these qualifiers. Why? Because those were less common names.

Looking at the names of Jesus's disciples in Matthew 10:2-4 we see a spot-on corollary between the most common names which always have a qualifier and the least common names with no qualifiers. This is a remarkable detail that no forger could have anticipated, but that a truthful witness couldn't help but provide to us.

So, the most common names—Simon, James, John, Matthew and Judas—all have qualifiers to distinguish them. The least common names—Andrew, Philip, Bartholomew, Thomas and Thaddaeus do not have qualifiers.

Dr. Williams, and many other New Testament scholars, are reasonably impressed that the Gospel writers got the names right. In their estimation, the fact that they remembered the names—a detail that most people find the most impossible to remember—and that they accurately record the frequency and types of names, suggests very strongly that they were careful to record everything else accurately as well.

Therefore, unlike the popular comparison to the telephone game, where children whisper a phrase from person to person until it is completely unintelligible from the original statement, we see the opposite. We see a Gospel record that retains very specific details about seemingly minor characters and accurately communicates their names, decades after the facts and thousands of miles away.

Dr. Williams suggests that the passing along of the details in the New Testament documents are more comparable to the art of Karate. "No one today suggests that the form of Karate we have today has been corrupted over time," he says. Instead, the fact that it has been carefully passed along from teacher to student for thousands of years has actually helped to maintain the integrity of the martial art so that the discipline we have today is very reasonably considered to be practically identical to the form practiced in the very beginning.

The accuracy of minor details doesn't end at the use of people's names. The Gospel authors are also aware of the names of several cities and villages in the area, and they speak of them with amazing expertise.

If people were writing stories about places they had never been, they wouldn't be able to name locations with much accuracy. "How would someone in Syria, or Greece or Italy know these details? If you found a book about another country it might include the names of the great cities you'd want to visit before you die, but it wouldn't include the names of obscure villages like Bethphage or Chorazin," says Williams. "The Gospel authors don't just know the names, they also know details about them. They know that Capernaum is next to the sea. They know whether the land in those areas goes up or down, they know traveling times, etc. How did they get that right?"

In contrast, Williams points out that the Gospels of Philip and Peter and Thomas only mention Jerusalem and Nazareth whereas the Gospels mention a total of 23 towns and villages.

"The non-canonical Gospels are in fact evidence for the accuracy of the four Gospels because they are examples of what would happen if someone did make up the details," says Williams. "How could Luke know that Zacchaeus climbed up in a sycamore tree?" asks Williams, pointing out that sycamore trees didn't even exist in the countries where the Gospels were eventually written down. They would have only known about those trees from eyewitnesses. "These are the sorts of details that people who have been to a place know. So, the Gospel writers get it right. Not just on place names or on people's names, but they're getting it right on botany, on the shape of houses, on the description of the Temple, they're getting the coinage right, they're getting the social stratification right, they're getting the religious setting right. After a while you think, there are so many opportunities for them to go wrong if they're making it up," he says. "But they don't seem to get it wrong."

This evidence strongly supports the idea that the authors of the canonical Gospels in the New Testament scriptures were reporting details accurately and those details could only have come from people who had lived in that time period and in that region. "For me this looks credible. This is not something that was made up by people somewhere far removed from the events," says Williams. "The sort of telephone game process that corrupts details doesn't discriminate. So, if the Gospel writers have correctly recorded the minor details, isn't it reasonable to think they could correctly report the major ones? If the Gospels were produced on a basis of stories several steps removed from the eyewitnesses, this [attention to detail] is not what you would expect."

So, are the Gospels reliable? This evidence certainly leans heavily in that direction.

But all this proves is that the Gospel writers were truthful and accurate. What about the letters of Paul, or the other New Testament documents? Can those also be trusted? Is it possible that some of those have been mistranslated or misunderstood over the centuries?

We'll look at that in our next chapter.

CHAPTER 13

WHEN BEING BIBLICALLY-RIGHT IS COMPLETELY WRONG

"When [LGBTQ-affirming Christians] tell me that I am wrong for saying that [homosexuality] is a sin, in the simplicity of my faith in the Holy Scriptures, I point him to this sacred record [the Bible], and tell him, in all candor, as my text does, that his teaching blasphemes the name of God and His doctrine.

"The tree of [affirming homosexuality and transgenderism] is evil and only evil...[it] is nourished by an utter rejection of the Scriptures."

— REV. HENRY VAN DYKE

Many Christians today would agree whole-heartedly with Pastor Van Dyke's statements here. But, surprisingly, what he was *actually* defending here was slavery (not homosexuality) and his opponents were Abolitionists. Still, his position in favor of slaveholding was very strongly supported by the Holy Scriptures. One cannot deny that he was right about the fact that the Bible did not condemn slaveholding outright.

But we cannot miss the fact that it is more than possible for someone to be Biblically-correct about something and still be very, very wrong at the same time.

The struggle for many of us is that we have been told for so long that we need to be "Biblically-minded" that we have forgotten that this same Bible teaches us to listen to the voice of the Good Shepherd and affirms that we have the mind of Christ.

> THE STRUGGLE FOR MANY OF US IS THAT WE HAVE BEEN TOLD FOR SO LONG THAT WE NEED TO BE "BIBLICALLY-MINDED" THAT WE HAVE FORGOTTEN THAT THIS SAME BIBLE TEACHES US TO LISTEN TO THE VOICE OF THE GOOD SHEPHERD AND AFFIRMS THAT WE HAVE THE MIND OF CHRIST.

Furthermore, the same Bible also teaches us to love extravagantly—as Christ has loved us—which was unconditionally and before we did anything to change our minds about Him, or how we live.

Here are Van Dykes actual comments about Abolitionists made in 1860:

"The tree of Abolition is evil and only evil…[it] is nourished by an utter rejection of the Scriptures…When the Abolitionist tells me that slaveholding is sin, in the simplicity of my faith in the Holy Scriptures, I point him to this sacred record, and tell him, in all candor, as my text does, that his teaching blasphemes the name of God and His doctrine." (Rev. Henry Van Dyke, *The Character and Influence of Abolitionism*, 1860, p.11)

Now, listen to what pro-slavery Christians said in the 1800's about Abolitionists and substitute the topic of homosexuality and you'll see that the arguments used today are exactly the same:

"[Opponents of slavery] decide a priori [in advance] what the Bible ought to speak, and then turn it over in order to see how they can make it speak what they wish…When Moses speaks the words of the God of the Hebrews, it is for us to listen, not to call into question." (Bernard Whitman, *Two Letters to the Rev. Moses Stuart: On the Subject of Religious Liberty*, 1831, p. 30-42)

"If the present course of the abolitionists is right, then the course of Christ and the apostles were wrong." (Charles Hodge, "Bible Argument on Slavery" in E.N. Elliott's *Cotton Is King*, 1860, p. 849)

"Those who oppose slavery are engaged in willful or conscious opposition to the truth...Who are we, that in our modern wisdom presume to set aside the Word of God, and...invent for ourselves a 'higher law' than those holy Scriptures which are given to us as 'a light to our feet and a lamp to our paths' must answer?" (Episcopal Bishop John Henry Hopkins, *Scriptural, Ecclesiastical, and Historical View of Slavery*, 1864, p.16)

Those who opposed slavery (the Abolitionists) had very little scriptural support for their position, but they were on the side of Christ all the same.

Why is it so hard for us today to see that there are times when we need to listen to the mind of Christ and the voice of the Good Shepherd in order to fulfill the law of love?

As Henry Brinton said recently:

"An answer based only on Biblical quotations may put us on the side of Southern theologians who supported slavery and lost their way." (Quoted from CNN, Oct. 15, 2014: John Blake, *How the Bible Was Used To Justify Slavery, Abolitionism.*)

Sometimes, to obey Jesus we might have to admit that the Bible falls short. In those cases, we must cling tightly to the Good Shepherd and remember His command:

"Love one another as I have loved you." (John 13:34)

Today, almost no Christian would argue in favor of slavery, in spite of the fact that it is quite "Biblical."

So, the question of "authority" immediately comes to mind. Some argue for the inerrant and infallible authority of Scripture as the rule for a Christian's life. But others, like me, suggest instead that our authority is Christ and that it is still the Holy Spirit who cries out to the Body of Christ today.

Sadly, many of us will not, or cannot, listen because we are convinced that our Bibles—and only our Bibles—have authority over us.

Are we willing to submit ourselves to the Holy Spirit? Are we courageous enough to allow Jesus to be our guide?

Keep in mind that the Bible never holds itself up as our final authority. Instead, the Bible points us to Jesus and reminds us that He is the Head of the Church.

In the words of our Abba Father who thundered from heaven, *"This is my Son. Listen to Him!"*

If we listen to Jesus, He will lead us to liberate our brothers and sisters from oppression. He will teach us not to hate anyone but to love everyone.

If we cling stubbornly to our Bibles, we are led to believe that God approves of genocide, slavery, patriarchy, polygamy, torture, war and many other pre-Christian ideas that Jesus calls us to abandon.

CHAPTER 14

THE BIBLE SAYS IT, BUT SHOULD YOU BELIEVE IT?

"You can know the Bible by heart and yet not know the heart of it."

— KENN STILGER

As we've already seen, sometimes there's a problem with taking scripture at face value. To merely point to a certain verse in our Bibles and proclaim that the sentences we read there are the end of the discussion is a big mistake.

Not only do we need to read the Bible through the lens of Christ, we also need to understand that our English translations of the scripture may not always reflect what is actually being communicated in the original text, nor may it fully convey the message that the original authors intended.

I'd like to point to two examples of where our Bibles may say one thing but the entire meaning has been obscured over time by a variety of factors.

First, let's look at a handful of verses in the epistles of Paul that appear, at first glance, to be unyielding commands against women speaking or teaching in the Church.

The passages that are most often used to silence women in the Body of Christ are:

"I do not permit a woman to teach or to have authority over a man; she must be silent." (1 Tim. 2:12)

"Women should remain silent in the churches. They are not allowed to speak, but must be in submission, as the law says. If they want to inquire about something, they should ask their own husbands at home; for it is disgraceful for a woman to speak in the church." (1 Cor. 14:34-35)

Again, taken at face value, these verses appear to render a decisive verdict. But there is much more going on in these passages than most realize. This is why we need to consider a few other factors before we close the case—or our minds—to what we might be missing.

For some, these verses end the discussion when it comes to the question of whether or not women can serve as leaders in the Church. They turn to these two verses, read them out loud and proclaim that women must be silent and that it is disgraceful for a woman to speak in the Church. That's the end of it.

But is it? Is this actually what Paul meant to communicate in these passages? Are we really understanding what is going on?

I used to think so. But then I realized that there were other things going on in these two verses that most of us are not aware of. One of my greatest discoveries was made when I read a great little book by Jon Zens called *What's with Paul and Women?*

In this book, Zens uncovers two main factors that we need to consider in greater detail. These are context and culture. As we'll see later, there is one other factor to consider, but we'll save that last one for the end.

For now, let's take the statement in 1 Timothy and look at the context. At the very beginning of the letter, Paul explains to Timothy that the reason he is writing to him is because there are "certain people" at the church in Ephesus who are teaching "false doctrines" and who "want to be teachers of the law, but they do not know what they are talking about." (See 1 Tim. 1:3-7)

Who are these "certain people"? We don't know them by name, but we can glean a few clues about who they were and what they were teaching based on other statements made by Paul later in the epistle, and by studying more about the city of Ephesus at the time this letter was written.

We can safely assume that at least one of those "certain people" who were "want[ing] to be teachers" was a woman because Paul says, "A woman should learn in quietness and full submission. I do not permit a woman to teach." (1 Tim. 2:11-12)

Paul refers to "a woman" who is not willing to learn and who wants to teach, specifically "...to assume authority over a man", adding "she must be quiet." (v. 12)

If you understood more about the culture of Ephesus, this problem with a certain woman would not be hard to accept as a by-product of the climate there.

Our first clue about what it was like in Ephesus at that time in history is found in Acts chapter 19. Here we read about what happened when Paul's preaching in that city resulted in the repentance of many who practiced sorcery and the public burning of occultic scrolls valued at fifty thousand drachmas. In response to this, a silversmith named Demetrius, who made silver shrines to the goddess Artemis (remember that detail for later), gathering other artisans in that city to protest the spread of the Gospel because, as he put it:

> "There is danger not only that our trade will lose its good name, but also that the temple of the great goddess Artemis will be discredited; and the goddess herself, who is worshiped throughout the province of Asia and the world, will be robbed of her divine majesty." (v. 27)

The response to this threat to their livelihood—and to the worship of Artemis—was unprecedented. The people became furious and began to shout "Great is Artemis of the Ephesians!" and eventually a large crowd of people joined them and they all began to shout in unison for two hours straight: "Great is Artemis of the Ephesians!" (v. 34)

So, as you might gather from this passage, people in Ephesus really loved Artemis. In fact, there was a temple to Artemis in that city which was called one of the seven wonders of the world by many. It was the central hub for worship to this goddess.

Big deal, you might say. What does that this have to do with what Paul says about women in 1 Timothy?

A lot. You see, Artemis worship was a female cult. That means it was led by female priests. Those women who worshipped Artemis did so primarily by adorning their hair with gold and jewels. They did so because Artemis promised to protect them—and their unborn children—through the often life-threatening process of childbirth.

By now, if you're at all familiar with the rest of what Paul says in 1 Timothy, these details are starting to connect a few dots for you. If not, don't worry, we'll explain those in short order.

The final detail about Artemis worship that might be helpful to us in understanding what Paul is saying in these verses is that they believed that women were created first, and men were created second.

Now, with this information in mind, let's re-examine what Paul is actually saying in 1 Timothy in light of what we know about the culture in Ephesus and the grip that Artemis worship had on the people who lived there.

As we mentioned, Paul begins his letter by pointing out that there are "certain people" in that Ephesian church who "want to be teachers" and that they want specifically to "assume authority over a man". Then, he quickly mentions that "a woman should learn in quietness and full submission" and adds, "I do not permit a woman to teach".

I would like to suggest that Paul has in mind a certain woman and that his statements here are directed to her and not necessarily to all women everywhere. But we'll explore that idea a bit later. For now, let's look at a few other sections of Paul's letter to Timothy that come into focus in light of what we now understand about Artemis worship.

Notice what Paul says in chapter 2:

"I also want the women to dress modestly, with decency and propriety, adorning themselves, not with elaborate hairstyles or gold or pearls or expensive clothes, but with good deeds, appropriate for women who profess to worship God." (v. 9-10)

Why would Paul stress that Christian women in Ephesus should not dress extravagantly or adorn themselves or wear elaborate hairstyles? Perhaps because he knows that this would give the appearance to others that those women were worshipping Artemis rather than God.

Perhaps this is also why Paul goes on to add:

"For Adam was formed first, then Eve. And Adam was not the one deceived; it was the woman who was deceived and became a sinner. But women will be saved through childbearing—if they continue in faith, love and holiness with propriety." (v. 13-15)

Do you see what's going on here? Paul is contrasting the teachings of Artemis with the teachings of Christianity. First, he reminds Timothy that, according to the Hebrew scriptures, it was man who was formed first, not the woman. His intention is to refute the teachings of Artemis which reverse this order, and then he says "women will be saved through child-bearing" because he wants to remind them that it is Jesus—not Artemis—who will protect them and their child when they give birth.

Doesn't that make so much more sense to you now? Those who are unaware of Artemis worship and what it involves tend to read these passages in the most outlandish ways possible. I've even heard some very wise theologians and Bible scholars interpret this passage to mean that women need to have children and that this in some strange way adds to their eternal security, which is of course ridiculous.

This is why I stress that we have to do more than just read the words in our English translations and declare that we have the entire story. We don't. There are often other factors going on that we are oblivious to. Without the full context and an awareness of the culture of that time period, we will never fully understand what is being said, or why.

> THIS IS WHY I STRESS THAT WE HAVE TO DO MORE THAN JUST READ THE WORDS IN OUR ENGLISH TRANSLATIONS AND DECLARE THAT WE HAVE THE ENTIRE STORY. WE DON'T. THERE ARE OFTEN OTHER FACTORS GOING ON THAT WE ARE OBLIVIOUS TO.

Once we understand the challenges facing the church in Ephesus—being centered in the very heart of a very strong culture of female-led Artemis worship—Paul's statements become clearer. We can see that, in this church, in this city, there were "certain people"—and more specifically "a woman"—who was trying to introduce concepts that were derived from Artemis worship into their gatherings. Because of this, Paul wanted to stress to Timothy, "I do not permit a woman to teach" and most specifically not to "gain authority over a man".

Another factor that adds to our misunderstanding of this passage relates to authority in general. Because many Christians today equate teaching with having authority over others in the Church. But nowhere in the scriptures are we ever told this. In fact, we are told that everyone in the Body of Christ needs to submit to one another (See Eph. 5:21) and so Paul wouldn't allow a man to teach or have authority over anyone in the Church either.

But, because many of us have been conditioned to believe that the teacher or the preacher is in authority over us, we therefore believe that if a woman teaches a man that she is in authority over him. This is not so.

If a woman teaches a man something from the scriptures, she is not in authority over him, the Holy Spirit is.

In other words, we do not submit to teachers per se. We all submit to one another in humility and mutual respect, and everyone in the Body of Christ is under submission to the Holy Spirit who leads all of us together into the Truth of the Gospel.

Now, while we're still in 1 Timothy we might also look quickly at another misunderstood verse about women and clarify that one before we move over to the verse in 1 Corinthians 14.

Later in 1 Timothy, Paul gives instructions about selecting overseers and deacons in the Church. Typically, these verses have been used to restrict women from serving in these capacities. But this is largely due to the mistranslation of a particular word in chapter 3 and by ignoring many other scriptures in the New Testament that strongly argue that women most certainly were allowed to serve as overseers and deacons.

The word that our English Bibles typically mistranslate is in verse 11 which reads:

> "In the same way, *the women* are to be worthy of respect, not malicious talkers but temperate and trustworthy in everything."

If your Bible is a King James, or ESV translation that same verse is translated like this:

> "Even so must *their wives* be grave, not slanderers, sober, faithful in all things."

See the difference one little word makes? By translating the word "women" as "their wives", the opportunity for a woman to become a deacon or an overseer is obliterated. And for many centuries this mistranslation of the word "women" to "their wives" kept millions of women from serving as deacons in the Christian church.

But this is not what the early Christians practiced. How do we know this? Because there are several mentions of women throughout the New Testament who are clearly identified as deacons and even some as evangelists, prophets and apostles.

For example:

"Greet Andronicus and Junia, my fellow Jews who have been in prison with me. They are outstanding among the apostles, and they were in Christ before I was." (Romans 16:7)

Note that Junia is a female name and that Paul calls both her and Andronicus "apostles". However, for centuries the Christian church renamed Junia to be "Junias" in order to make her appear male. Why would they do that? To prevent anyone from challenging their views that women should be silent in the church. It's only in recent times that New Testament scholars have restored her femininity and yet the tradition of male-centered leadership in the Body of Christ remains the norm.

The New Testament also mentions Priscilla and Aquila several times, usually listing the wife, Priscilla, first. As men were traditionally mentioned first, the practice of listing the wife first, in this case, is a strong indication of her prominence over her husband. It was not a matter of etiquette. It was a very purposeful way for Paul to indicate that Priscilla was the more gifted one between the two of them.

Additionally, Paul, when speaking of this couple says, "Greet Priscilla and Aquila, my co-workers in Christ Jesus." (Romans

16:3) which puts them on an equal level with Paul and suggests that they were both doing Apostolic work, the same as he was.

This couple even took another Apostle (Apollos) into their home to teach him about the baptism of the Holy Spirit and to pray for him to receive it, (and he did).

So, this couple was not only doing apostolic work, like Paul was doing, but they were even ministering to other Apostles and laying hands on them to be filled with the Spirit of God. They also hosted a church in their home, so we know that they were church planters and servants in the local Christian community.

Therefore, there should be no doubt that women in the early New Testament church served as Apostles.

Another example of a female deacon and elder is Phoebe whom Paul refers to as "a servant of the Church"—literally "*diakonos*" in the Greek, or "deacon". (See Romans 16:1)

Paul also mentions Euodia and Syntyche in Philippians 4, as well as Tabitha and Dorcas in Acts 9 and calls them "diakonos" or deacons.

We also have examples of women prophesying in the New Testament church—which would make them prophets—as Paul gives clear instructions as to how women should prophesy:

> "But every woman who prays or prophesies with her head uncovered dishonors her head." (1 Cor. 11:5)

Paul's only concern here is how women are dressed when they prophesy in the Church, not whether or not they prophesy. In fact, he assumes that both men and women will be doing so. Which brings us to the next verse about silencing women in the Church found in the same letter to the Corinthians.

The verse that many use as the final word on this question of women teaching in the Church is found here:

"Women should remain silent in the churches. They are not allowed to speak, but must be in submission, as the law says. If they want to inquire about something, they should ask their own husbands at home; for it is disgraceful for a woman to speak in the church." (1 Cor. 14:34-35)

I will admit, this appears pretty devastating at first glance. But we need to apply context and culture as we've already demonstrated. So, let's see if we can shed some light on this passage.

First, let's admit that this statement appears quite out of character for Paul, especially in light of what we've already read about how he takes the time to honor women as fellow-apostles and deacons and prophets in the Church. Not to mention how Paul—in this very same letter—has taken the time to argue that women should prophesy out loud in their gatherings together, as long as their heads are covered.

So, why has Paul suddenly changed his mind and decided that women should not only "remain silent in the churches" but that "it is disgraceful for a woman to speak in the church"?

Has he lost his mind? Why the sudden about-face?

Here's what we often misunderstand about 1 Corinthians: It's not the first letter to the Corinthians.

In chapter 5 Paul refers to another letter that he wrote to them—which we do not have a copy of—and reminds them:

"I wrote to you in my letter not to associate with sexually immoral people—not at all meaning the people of this world who are immoral...In that case you would have to leave this world." (1 Cor. 5:9-10)

His next statement says, *"But now I am writing to you..."* (v. 11) so we know that this is at least his second letter to them, not his first.

What we also need to understand is that they wrote a letter to him in response to his first letter—which we also do not have a copy of. (See 1 Cor. 7:1)

Therefore, what we now call 1 Corinthians is actually Paul's response to their letter to him where they apparently asked him several questions about worship, controversy in their fellowship, and other questions that we can only guess at.

Reading 1 Corinthians is a little like listening to one side of a telephone conversation where you can only hear one person's responses and not what the person on the other end is saying.

READING 1 CORINTHIANS IS A LITTLE LIKE LISTENING TO ONE SIDE OF A TELEPHONE CONVERSATION WHERE YOU CAN ONLY HEAR ONE PERSON'S RESPONSES AND NOT WHAT THE PERSON ON THE OTHER END IS SAYING.

Because of this, many scholars believe that Paul is responding to their letter point-by-point and often-times referencing what they said to him before rendering his answers.

This is why in 1 Corinthians 14:34-35 we read a paragraph that appears to be completely contradictory to everything else that Paul has just said previously about women prophesying in the gatherings and statements about how everyone should use their spiritual gifts to edify one another, and other inconsistencies.

What also makes this challenging to determine exactly is that Greek, (the original language Paul's epistle was written in), doesn't contain punctuation marks. So, we have no idea exactly when Paul might be quoting their letter and when he might be responding to their questions.

Another huge clue about what might be happening in 1 Corinthians is the missing word in chapter 14.

Yes, that's right. Most English translations leave out an entire word that follows directly after the controversial statements about women being silent and disgraceful when they speak.

Here's the missing word: *"What?!"* In the Greek it's simply the letter ἤ, but the common usage is consistent with an exclamation of disbelief, and this word is omitted in most modern English translations.

That's right. Modern Bible translators have intentionally left out this exclamation by Paul following that scandalous paragraph. Why would they do that? Perhaps because, when taken all together, the section reads like this:

> "Women should remain silent…it is a disgrace for a woman to speak in the Church."

> "*WHAT?!* So, did the word of God originate with you? Are you the only ones who can hear His voice? If you think you're a prophet or gifted by the Spirit then admit that what I've written to you in this letter is the Lord's command."

That one little word changes everything, doesn't it? Now we can see that Paul stands by his earlier statements about women prophesying freely and using their gifts to encourage their brothers and sisters in the Body. He very clearly challenges them to decide if they're going to abide by his instructions or by their own ideas about women.

What's more, we can safely argue that the paragraph in question is not written by Paul because there are several clues. For example, Paul wrote extensively about the Law and contrasted it with the Gospel of Grace. Therefore it makes no sense that Paul would have appealed to the law as a standard for how the Corinthians should behave in the Church.

So, the statement *"Women should remain silent in the churches. They are not allowed to speak, but must be in submission, as the law says"* isn't something that Paul would have said.

Not only this, but the law doesn't say anything about women remaining silent or not being allowed to speak. Paul, who was trained as a Pharisee, would certainly have been aware of this fact and therefore would never have argued that the law forbids something if it didn't actually forbid it. Secondly, the paragraph also says:

> "…it is disgraceful for a woman to speak in the church."

If the law doesn't say this, and if we're reasonably sure that Paul didn't say it, then where did these ideas come from? The Talmud.[1]

As New Testament scholar Gordon Fee points out, the "law" here is most likely a reference to oral Jewish Law, or the Talmud which states:

> "It is a shame for a woman to let her voice be heard among men…the voice of a woman is filthy nakedness"

So, this is why we must be careful whenever we want to flip open our Bibles, point to a verse and claim that "The Bible clearly says" anything at all.

We first have to understand the context of the statement and do our best to understand the culture that the statement was made in before we attempt to apply those scriptures to ourselves, or to one another, today.

The third element I mentioned at the beginning of this chapter is translation bias, and we've already seen what it can do when a word is eliminated from our texts—like "What?!" in 1 Corinthians 14—or when a word is mistranslated—as in the word "women" becoming "their wives" in 1 Timothy, or "Junia" becoming a male in Romans 16:7.

Why are these verses "adjusted" in this way? What is the purpose? What agenda do they serve?

Clearly, our English scriptures are not without error, and some of those errors are carefully inserted to support power structures and traditions which have stood for centuries.

The subjugation of women in the Body of Christ is sad, but it's not the only example of cultural blindness and translation bias being used to silence and oppress a group of people.

The exact same thing happens when we look at the verses regarding homosexuality.

We read the verses in our English Bibles that clearly condemn homosexuals, but we are unaware that not all of those words are being fairly translated, and we are oblivious to the actual context of the verses themselves. This leads us to misunderstanding and it justifies the oppression and demonization of people for whom those verses really have no direct connection.

> **WE READ THE VERSES IN OUR ENGLISH BIBLES THAT CLEARLY CONDEMN HOMOSEXUALS, BUT WE ARE UNAWARE THAT NOT ALL OF THOSE WORDS ARE BEING FAIRLY TRANSLATED, AND WE ARE OBLIVIOUS TO THE ACTUAL CONTEXT OF THE VERSES THEMSELVES.**

Let's look at those verses in the same way that we looked at the verses regarding women and see if the same problems aren't apparent to us.

The typical "clobber verses" when it comes to homosexuality are the first chapter of Romans and 1 Corinthians 6:9.

Let's start with Romans 1:18 to try to understand what Paul is really talking about here. I think it helps to actually start "from the top", as it were.

In verse 18, Paul starts to talk about a group of people and this is how he identifies them:

> "The wrath of God is being revealed from heaven against all the godlessness and wickedness of people, who suppress the truth by their wickedness…"

Who is he talking about here? He's talking about "godless" and "wicked" people, in general.

In v. 21 he says those same people's thinking, "became futile and their foolish hearts were darkened".

Then he says in v. 22 that those same people "claimed to be wise but became fools".

And in v. 23 he says that they:

> "exchanged the glory of the immortal God for images made to look like a mortal human being and birds and animals and reptiles."

That is idol worship. In summary, these wicked and godless people denied the knowledge of God and began to worship idols.

Because of this:

> "Therefore God gave them over in the sinful desires of their hearts to sexual impurity for the degrading of their bodies with one another." (v.24)

So, because they denied God and worshipped idols God's response was to give them over to "shameful desires of their hearts…for the degrading of their bodies with one another."

Please Note: Sexual intercourse in pagan temples was quite common in the worship of idols. This is what Paul is referring to here, and he continues to describe this in verse 25:

> "They exchanged the truth about God for a lie, and worshiped and served created things rather than the Creator—who is forever praised."

This is all about idol worship and it involved sexual intercourse. What Paul is condemning here is the use of sexual intercourse as part of the worship of created things, or idols.

Now, Paul continues his progressive thought by saying, in verse 26:

> "Because of this, God gave them over to shameful lusts."

Ok, wait…because of what? Because these people, who were engaged in worshipping idols, started degrading their bodies with one another in ritual sexual intercourse: "God gave them over to shameful lusts."

So far, this would be bad no matter if the sex were gay or straight. Lust is lust, regardless of orientation.

There's a lot more to point out, but let me pause here just a moment to say this: I don't know anyone who is gay due to the effects of worshipping idols through sexual intercourse. Do you?

Maybe those people exist, but I would venture to say that the majority of people who identify as being gay today did not end up that way because they used to engage in pagan sexual practices in the temples of Zeus or Artemis.

I don't even know any gay people who feel attracted to people of the same sex due to denying that God exists. In fact, just the opposite, I know many people who identify as gay who profess saving faith in Christ and who even demonstrate the heart and character of Christ. They do not engage in "shameful desires of their hearts" any more than my straight Christian friends do. They also do not "worship and serve created things rather than the Creator".

Having said that, let's go back to Paul and continue the study. After this Paul says,

"Even their women exchanged natural sexual relations for unnatural ones. In the same way the men also abandoned natural relations with women and were inflamed with lust for one another. Men committed shameful acts with other men, and received in themselves the due penalty for their error."

Please try to follow the flow of Paul's statements here: There were people who denied God. They started to worship idols. That worship involved sexual intercourse. That intercourse aroused unnatural lusts. The end result was a judgment within their bodies for denying God and engaging in pagan ritual sex rites.

Keep in mind: anyone who is "inflamed with lust" is in sin - whether gay or straight. But Paul's entire flow of thought begins with a discussion about those who deny God, worship created things rather than the creator, engage in ritual sexual intercourse as part of that worship, and then—because of these things—God has judged them and given them over to their lusts.

Let me ask you: What if Paul's descriptions here went like this:

- People denied God

- Those people worshipped idols

- They worshipped idols by engaging in heterosexual acts

Would you conclude from this that God hated and condemned heterosexual intercourse?

Why not? Perhaps because we don't make the same assumptions about straight sex?

But, if we don't read Romans 1 as a de facto condemnation of straight sex—and the majority of the chapter is about straight sex—then why do we read it as a condemnation of gay intercourse?

Could it be because we have a bias against gay people that we don't have against straight people?

If we lay aside our inherent bias against gay sex, we can see that Paul's entire point is that the denial of God and the worship of idols through sexual intercourse (gay or straight) is what is "shameful" and not the type of sexual intercourse itself.

Sexual intercourse in the worship of idols is evil. This is Paul's entire point. Straight sex is not evil. What matters is the context. Is it between two people who love one another and who also love and trust in God? If so, then it is not what Paul is speaking of in Romans 1.

My point is simply this: Romans doesn't try to provide any commentary on whether or not gay sexual intercourse is "good" or "evil".

Paul's purpose in Romans isn't to explain why homo/hetero sex itself is wrong or right. His point would be exactly the same if he were describing straight sexual intercourse used in pagan ritual worship.

That same judgment they received would come equally to those who engaged in gay or straight sexual intercourse if it was for the purpose of pagan idol worship.

Believe it or not, there really are Christians who *are* gay, and they *do* worship God and they *do* love Jesus and they do *not* engage in fornication and they are *not* consumed by their lusts.

So, this passage does not apply to them. Next, let's examine 1 Corinthians 6:9-10 which says:

> "Or do you not know that the unrighteous will not inherit the kingdom of God? Do not be deceived; neither fornicators, nor idolaters, nor adulterers, nor effeminate, nor homosexuals, nor thieves, nor the covetous, nor drunkards, nor revilers, nor swindlers, will inherit the kingdom of God."

That seems pretty clear, but as we've already seen in the case of scriptures against women, there's probably more going on here than meets the eye.

Before we get into this, let's try to understand something about the way Paul thought about things from a first century context.

In the New Testament scriptures, the Apostle Paul speaks out against a trend that he sees as being "unnatural" and an "abomination" and warns that Christians need to be on their guard against this dangerous practice.

What is it? Well, it might surprise you. See, in Paul's day being a man meant keeping your hair short and your beard long.

Why? Because women had long hair and smooth faces. So, to Paul—and many others in his day—if a man had long hair and shaved his beard off, he was accused of "going against nature."

The Greek word Paul uses to describe this trend is "malakoi" and the best translation of the word into English is "effeminate".

In the first century, "malakoi" was most often used to reference men who shaved daily and had no beards. These men were often ridiculed and accused of wanting to look like women with clean-shaven faces.

This term was used as an epithet against men who are not masculine enough, as in, "You punch like a girl."

Plato, for example, in his "Republic", wrote famously that "too much music made a man soft [malakoi], and feeble; unfit for battle."

Aristotle also warned about the dangers of men becoming too soft (malakoi) by over-indulging in pleasures rather than balancing out their lives with acts of physical and mental discipline.

Even Josephus, the first century Jewish historian (and contemporary of Jesus and Paul) used the term "malakos" to describe men who were weak and soft through lack of courage in battle.

So, the word "malakoi" refers to being "soft", rather than masculine, and it occurs four times, in three verses in the New Testament. (Jesus even uses the same word to refer to soft clothing, for example, in Matthew 11:8 and Luke 7:25).

Now, here's the problem: the term "malakoi" is the word that is translated in most English Bibles today as "homosexual".

Let me ask you: Do you think that a man who shaves his beard and has long hair and enjoys music is a homosexual? Is he an abomination? Is he going against his nature? Hopefully not.

But even so, we need to understand that when Paul uses the term "malakoi" he is not referring to someone who is a homosexual. So, when our English Bibles translate "soft" as "homosexual" this is an error and it is not an accidental one.

The word "malakoi" is never used to refer to someone who is homosexual by anyone in the first century. Yet, it is often used to describe a heterosexual male whose behavior is more feminine, or "soft".

So, to determine what Paul had in mind in 1 Cor. 6:9 we need to go to the actual Greek language which reads:

> "Know ye not that the unrighteous shall not inherit the kingdom of God? Be not deceived: neither fornicators, nor idolaters, nor adulterers, nor effeminate, nor abusers of themselves with mankind.." (1 Cor. 6:9)

But the definition of "effeminate" is not the same today as it was in the first century, is it?

Back then it was "unnatural" for a man to shave his face and grow a mullet. Today, mullets still aren't so popular, but we wouldn't say that a person who sported one was "unrighteous" and unwelcome in the Kingdom of God.

The term "effeminate" is based on a cultural bias, not an absolute law of scripture.

If you want to make it an absolute statement, then we must adopt Paul's first century ideals about what makes a man "effeminate" and that means that all men are forbidden to shave their beards or wear their hair below their ears to be considered godly. It also means that women can't wear pants, or cut their hair short.

So, do we all want to adopt Paul's ideas about cultural norms? Are we willing to live by this rule?

> "Doth not even nature itself teach you, that, if a man have long hair, it is a shame unto him? But if a woman have long hair, it is a glory to her: for her hair is given her for a covering." (1 Cor. 11:14-15)

The fact is, only the most legalistic Christians still hold to these rules. Most of us have accepted that this verse is an example of Paul's cultural expectations of what was acceptable and what wasn't. If we're not willing to abide by these rules today, then we cannot condemn the effeminate or those who shave their beards to eternal destruction.

So, unless we honestly believe that a man with a clean-shaven face is an abomination to God and that guys with long hair are excluded from the Kingdom of God, then we need to rethink our views on homosexuality, too.

> SO, UNLESS WE HONESTLY BELIEVE THAT A MAN WITH A CLEAN-SHAVEN FACE IS AN ABOMINATION TO GOD AND THAT GUYS WITH LONG HAIR ARE EXCLUDED FROM THE KINGDOM OF GOD, THEN WE NEED TO RETHINK OUR VIEWS ON HOMOSEXUALITY, TOO.

Another point worth making about those references in Romans chapter 1 and 1 Corinthians chapter 6 is this:

> "[Romans 1] builds a crescendo of condemnation, declaring God's wrath upon human unrighteousness, using rhetoric characteristic of Jewish polemic against Gentile immorality. It whips the reader into a frenzy of indignation against others: those unbelievers, those idol-worshippers, those immoral enemies of God. But then the sting strikes in Romans 2:1 'Therefore you have no excuse, whoever you are, when you judge others; for in passing judgment on another you condemn yourself because you, the judge, are doing the very same things."[2]

This observation about what Paul appears to really be up to in Romans chapter 1 is also apparent in 1 Corinthians chapter 6 where Paul, after listing all "those people" won't inherit the Kingdom of God, reminds his listeners:

> " And such were some of you. But you were washed, you were sanctified, you were justified in the name of the Lord Jesus Christ and by the Spirit of our God." (1 Cor. 6:11)

In both examples the intended result is the same: Paul seeks to reverse the self-righteous indignation of his audience against "sinners" by reminding them that they are just the same. His hope is that they might repent of their hateful attitudes towards others and find some compassion in their hearts for those they previously delighted in condemning to the wrath of God.

Our response to these verses where Paul lists the sorts of people who are unworthy of God's mercy is to see ourselves there, too. We should recognize that the entire point he's trying to make is that all of us have sinned and fallen short of God's glory, but the grace of God has been poured out on all of us. Rather than judge others, we should seek to see them as people, like us, who are dearly loved by God and recipients of His invitation to receive unmerited favor.

So, if we are committed to a more "Biblical" worldview, then we must accept that evils like slavery and genocide and patriarchy are somehow acceptable to God. But if we are convinced that Jesus is the perfect revelation of God, then we need to get busy learning how to love one another as Christ has loved us.

CHAPTER 15

BUT WHAT ABOUT...?

"Sometimes the Bible in the hands of one man is worse than a whiskey bottle in the hand of another."

— HARPER LEE, *TO KILL A MOCKINGBIRD*

As I prepared to write this book I posted a few thoughts on my blog and what followed was a very robust dialog about this new way of reading the Scriptures.

Here are some honest questions that you may also find yourself asking after reading this far. Hopefully these answers can help you process everything.

"Everything you're saying comes from the Bible. You wouldn't even know Jesus if it wasn't for the Scriptures!"

Yes, I get that. I really do. But just because I got this information from the Book, doesn't mean I disregard the information.

In other words, the Book tells me to cling to Jesus, to know Jesus, to draw near to Jesus and to abide in Jesus.

Do I cling to the Book, know the Book, draw near to the Book and abide in the Book because I read something in the Book?

Would that make any sense?

This response above is one I have heard hundreds of times: "We can't know Jesus apart from the Bible."

But this isn't the truth. We are told—by the Book—that we can know Jesus by His Spirit that lives inside of us. He reveals Himself to us daily if we abide in Him and learn to listen for His still, small voice.

This attitude—that we can't know Jesus apart from the Scriptures—also reveals that many have found Jesus in a Book and stopped right there.

My hope is to show them that Jesus may have been *introduced* to them in a Book, but the real, living, breathing *Jesus* is too big and too marvelous to be limited by that Book.

He wants us to know Him intimately and to learn how to hear His voice—because He said we could if we were His sheep—and He wants to come and make His home in us. He wants us to learn to hear the voice of the Holy Spirit who leads us into all Truth.

The idea that we must cling to the Bible because this is how we first heard of Jesus is irrational.

For example, I met my wife Wendy through our mutual friend, Carlos. Should I spend all of my time with Carlos now?

"But, Keith, you wouldn't even know your wife if it wasn't for Carlos!"

Yes, this is true. I do love my friend Carlos, very much. But I did not fall in love with Carlos in the same way that I am in love with Wendy. So, while I am very grateful to Carlos for introducing me to Wendy, my relationship with Wendy is much more profound, and deep.

Sadly, many Christians have fallen in love with the Scriptures that point them to Christ rather than listening to those Scriptures that tell us to fall in love with Jesus.

Over and over again that Book urges us to mature in our relationship with a living God—not a Book. So, if we really, truly believe that Book then let's do what it says. Let's take what it says seriously.

WHAT MANY HAVE TODAY, SADLY, IS A RELIGION BASED ON A BOOK. BUT WHAT GOD WANTS—AND HAS *ALWAYS* WANTED—IS AN ONGOING RELATIONSHIP WITH HIS PEOPLE.

In other words, the Book doesn't point us to the Book. The Book points us to the Word of God who was made flesh, and who now wants to live and breathe within His people.

What many have today, sadly, is a religion based on a Book. But what God wants—and has *always* wanted—is an ongoing relationship with His people.

"Why should we believe "God is perfect, and Jesus perfectly reveals the Father to us" when you say "The Bible is not perfect. The Scriptures are not error-free"? Perhaps the parts of the Bible that lead you to believe "Jesus perfectly reveals the Father to us" are erroneous and uninspired writings? Who's to say what's inspired and correct in the Bible and what's not? You? Me? Is it the Church? Is it the voice of Jesus? Who's to say when the voice of Jesus is inspired and correct and when it's not? The Bible? The Church? Since the Bible contradicts itself, shouldn't we expect the Church and the voice of Jesus to contradict themselves, too? Seems like you're throwing the Bible out with the 'flat Bible perspective' bath water. I can't see any good coming from your approach, here, to the Bible: "In fact, there are errors, mistakes and contradictions all through it.""

I know that this approach to the scriptures provokes all sorts of questions. Perhaps this is why we call it "faith" and not "certainty". The opposite of "faith" is "certainty", not "doubt".

As I've shown, the Bible is not error-free. We shouldn't pretend it is. There is no power in that, nor is there any honesty or truth to it.

Our Bible is flawed. Just like the people who wrote it. Yet God still loves to pour His Spirit into us, in spite of this.

Who's to say what is inspired or not?

Well, each of us who abides in Christ has the Holy Spirit living within—the actual "Word of God" dwells inside of us. So, we can use discernment when we read the scriptures—or anything else—to determine what is true or not true.

This is exactly what Jesus promised the Holy Spirit would do: "He will lead you into all Truth" This is a gift directly from our Lord. Let's learn how to use this gift as He intended.

But isn't this dangerous? What if we get it wrong?

Can we get it wrong? Of course we can. But we can—and we do—get it very wrong even when we assume the Bible is inerrant. So, there's really no difference between the two approaches on that end, is there?

Whether you assume the Bible is perfect or not, there is still the chance to get it wrong—or to get it right.

So, yes, the Bible does contradict itself—at times. But, not always. I have pointed out a few examples here, but this doesn't mean the entire Bible is always contradictory. I have not said this, nor do I believe it.

When it comes to what we know of Christ, I see no contradictions. Yes, there are a few minor contradictions regarding the specific details of the resurrection, but all agree that it happened.

The strongest evidence for the resurrected Christ is the boldness of the disciples, the empty tomb and the failure of Rome or the Jewish leaders to produce the body to silence those who testified that He was alive.

I would caution you, and everyone who follows Christ, not to put your hope or your faith in a Bible that cannot be wrong, but in a Christ who is faithful and true.

If your hope is in a perfect Bible, then it's all-too-easy to poke holes in that foundation. But if your hope is in a perfectly true Jesus who reveals the Father and has the words of life, you'll never be disappointed. That, I can guarantee.

Doesn't consistency require that we view the words of Jesus recorded in the New Testament not as words of God but early Christians' understanding of Him?

The only way we know that the Old Testament view of God is "off" is because it doesn't square up with the clearest picture anyone has ever had of God who was—and is—Christ.

If our understanding of Christ is based on the early Christians' understanding of him, then so be it. But let's look at the fruit of their lives as the result of this understanding: Sharing all things in common, loving the poor, the widow and the outcast as their own flesh and blood, radical nonviolence in the face of persecution and death, etc. Look at how beautiful and Christ-like their lives were in comparison to our own. Isn't this what we aspire to? Shouldn't we do whatever we can to move ourselves closer to that ideal of loving as Jesus loved and giving as Jesus gave?

What about the violence we see from Jesus in the book of Revelation [where] Jesus is the Lamb, whose wrath is displayed in the horrors that befell Jerusalem in AD 70—which even included women eating their own children?

I would point out the difference between predicting the fruit of the Jewish rebellion and their failure to "learn the things that make for peace" (as Jesus wept over Jerusalem in His triumphal entry) and actually causing the effect directly.

Yes, Jesus knew that the Jewish people would be destroyed if they did not repent of their desire to overthrow Roman rule. He warned them of this many times. Unfortunately, those who did not heed this warning were, indeed, destroyed by the fruit of their own rebellion.

WHAT LITERALLY HAPPENED WAS THAT HE WARNED THEM, THEY IGNORED HIM, AND THEN THEY SUFFERED THE FATE THAT HE PREDICTED WOULD BEFALL THEM.

I would also argue that saying "God will cast you into the fires of Gehenna..." is apocalyptic hyperbole, not literal. I would say that God did not cast anyone anywhere.

People who refused to listen to Jesus suffered the fate that He predicted they would suffer. In that way, yes, it could be said that "God cast them into the fires of Gehenna" but only indirectly. What literally happened was that He warned them, they ignored Him, and then they suffered the fate that He predicted would befall them.

"Jesus believed in both the flood and the destruction of Sodom and Gomorrah, didn't He?"

I would say that this is like saying that Christians believe in the Prodigal Son and the Rich Man and Lazarus. Did Jesus teach these things? Yes. Does that mean that they were literal events? No, not necessarily.

Does that mean that those stories are not valuable and instructive to us today? Of course not. Many of those Old Testament stories may very well be true, but this is not the point. Jesus quoted those stories to teach something and this does not necessarily mean that He believed they were literal events.

No, Jesus did not take the opportunity to argue with the Jewish people about their stories being literal events or not, but we should realize that many Jewish teachers contend that those Old Testament stories were never *meant* to be taken as literal historic events, but were always seen more as parables that contained important lessons.

For example, many other cultures have a flood story. Many of those flood stories predate the version in our Old Testament scriptures. This does not mean that the story of Noah is not true. But what we should realize is that all those other cultures told their flood stories to prove that the gods were angry and that if we didn't appease them they would destroy us.

The Jewish version changes a few details to make an important, new point about Yahweh God. Namely, that He promised never to do such a thing ever again. This may be more important than whether or not it actually happened.

Every ancient culture told stories to explain how they saw their world and who they thought their god was. This is also why I reject certain views of God found in the Old Covenant Scriptures because they conflict with what Jesus reveals to us about the Father, and, as I have already shown, Jesus is the best and clearest picture anyone could ever have of what the Father actually looks like.

You might say that, if Jesus agreed with my thesis then He should have pointed these things out in His ministry here. To that point I like to say that several times when Jesus is correcting or contradicting the Old Testament Scriptures He often uses phrases like "*Your* scriptures say…" (not "God's scriptures"?) and "*Moses* said…" (but not "God said"?).

To me, this suggests that Jesus did not always necessarily affirm that everything written in the Old Testament was necessarily an historic event. His point seems to be more about how we live our lives based on how we see God. Many times Jesus encourages us to behave a certain way because to do so is to be like our Father in Heaven. (See Matt. 5:45)

This is not to say that the entire Old Testament is to be doubted. Far from it. I do believe that Jesus is glimpsed many times throughout the Hebrew scriptures. Many, if not most, of those scriptures reveal to us a God whose love endures forever and who is abounding in mercy and who calls us to care for the poor and the widow, etc.

However, I would simply say that, when seen through the lens of Christ, not everything we read in the Old Testament scriptures accurately reflects back to us the light of Christ that is shining upon it.

What the scriptures do perfectly and without error is to point us to Christ. Christ is the Truth. He is the Word of God made flesh. Let's follow Him and listen to Him.

"CERTAIN PEOPLE DECLARED IN MY HEARING, 'UNLESS I CAN FIND A THING IN OUR ANCIENT RECORDS, I REFUSE TO BELIEVE IT IN THE GOSPEL'; AND WHEN I ASSURED THEM THAT IT IS INDEED IN THE ANCIENT SCRIPTURES, THEY RETORTED, 'THAT HAS GOT TO BE PROVED'. BUT FOR MY PART, MY RECORDS ARE JESUS CHRIST; FOR ME, THE SACROSANCT RECORDS ARE HIS CROSS AND DEATH AND RESURRECTION, AND THE FAITH THAT COMES THROUGH HIM.

"THE PRIESTS OF OLD, I ADMIT, WERE ESTIMABLE MEN; BUT OUR OWN HIGH PRIEST IS GREATER, FOR HE HAS BEEN ENTRUSTED WITH THE HOLY OF HOLIES, AND TO HIM ALONE ARE THE SECRET THINGS OF GOD COMMITTED. HE IS THE DOORWAY TO THE FATHER, AND IT

IS BY HIM THAT ABRAHAM AND ISAAC
AND JACOB AND THE PROPHETS GO IN,
NO LESS THAN THE APOSTLES AND THE
WHOLE CHURCH; FOR ALL THESE HAVE
THEIR PART IN GOD'S UNITY.

"NEVERTHELESS, THE GOSPEL HAS
A DISTINCTION ALL ITS OWN, IN THE
ADVENT OF OUR SAVIOR JESUS CHRIST,
AND HIS PASSION AND RESURRECTION.
WE ARE FOND OF THE PROPHETS, AND
THEY DID INDEED POINT FORWARD TO
HIM IN THEIR PREACHING; YET IT IS THE
GOSPEL THAT SETS THE COPING-STONE
ON MAN'S IMMORTALITY. IT IS IN ALL
THESE DIFFERENT ELEMENTS TOGETHER
THAT GOODNESS RESIDES, IF YOU HAVE
A LOVING FAITH."

—IGNATIUS[1]

CHAPTER 16

BLIND SPOT BIAS

"Ever notice how everyone who drives slower than you is an idiot and everyone who drives faster than you is a maniac?"

— GEORGE CARLIN

Whenever we look out at the world, everything registers on our retina except for one area known as the blind spot. When it comes to perceiving reality, the biggest and most common blind spot is our self.

This little observation perfectly describes the blind spot that almost everyone suffers from. Those who agree with us are rational, intelligent and possibly even genius-level savants, but those who disagree with us are morons, buffoons, and sheeple.

This phenomenon—known as "Naïve Realism"—was observed and categorized by two scientists, Lee Ross and Andrew Ward, back in 1995.

They concluded that since most people believe that their ideas and opinions have only been arrived at after careful and thoughtful study, (which isn't usually true), we then falsely assume that a simple statement of facts which support our position will "fix" anyone who disagrees with us. When it doesn't work we then assume that these people must be idiots, blinded by their worldview, brain-washed, or possibly even subversive agents who oppose "The Truth", (which is also usually not true either).

Essentially, we all fail to recognize our own biases and, at the same time, are acutely aware of everyone else's biases.

Jesus called it having a log in the eye.

Naive Realism has three tenets:

One: You tend to believe that you arrived at your opinions after careful, rational analysis.

Two: Since you are devoted to sticking to the facts, this must mean that you are free from bias. Anyone who reads what you have read or experienced the same things you have will naturally see things your way.

Three: If anyone disagrees with your opinions it must be because they simply don't have all the facts yet.

Simply put, this is why we have so many arguments on the internet.

You read something and disagree with it. The other person cuts and pastes from their sources to prove you wrong or to defend their logic. You cut and paste, or quote from, your favorite sources to advance your unbiased perspective. They ignore that and post links to other sources that should convince you— if you were rational and unbiased as they are—and when it doesn't convince you they begin to go down their list of reasons why you must be so blind—you're stupid, you're brain-washed, you're lazy, etc.

Eventually someone gets un-friended or blocked.

Post. Argue. Repeat.

The problem comes when we assume that we see the world objectively, as it truly is. Therefore, we assume that those who see it otherwise are not simply seeing it differently, they are seeing it incorrectly.

We are right. They are wrong. That's all there is to it. But that isn't reality.

See, none of us is without bias. We all believe that our beliefs are the right beliefs—otherwise we'd believe something else. But if we're honest, we are much more critical of other people's arguments than we are of our own. Which is what a recent study discovered.

In the experiment conducted by Professor Lee Ross, University students were asked if they would be willing to walk around campus wearing a large wooden sign. About half of them agreed to do so. When asked to guess about how many others might also choose to wear the sign, or not wear the sign, both groups guessed that "a majority" of other students must have decided to do as they had done (Actual results were 50/50).

Then, they asked both groups this question: "For those who chose differently than you did, what do you think their choices reveal about them?"

In each case, students said that those who chose not to do as they had done were probably fearful, foolish, or otherwise abnormal. However, when asked what their own choices revealed about themselves, every student felt that their decisions revealed nothing about them; because they had simply made the "normal" choice that any rational person would have made.

Or, in other words, those who drive faster than me are maniacs and those who drive slower than me are idiots, but those who drive the same way I do are normal, rational and wonderful human beings.[1]

So, now that we're aware that we all do this, what can we do to mitigate against it?

Well, mainly it means that we have to recognize that we are not perfect. We are capable of being wrong. We all have our own inner bias, and we need to have grace for others who also have their own set of biases.

In our house church family, we've come to the same conclusions through other methods, but the essential concept is the same: We're all in process.

> **BECAUSE WE ALL RECOGNIZE THAT WE ARE IN PROCESS, ALONG WITH EVERYONE ELSE, WE TEND TO HAVE GRACE FOR ONE ANOTHER, ESPECIALLY FOR THOSE WHO DON'T HAPPEN TO SEE THINGS THE WAY WE CURRENTLY SEE THEM—BECAUSE NOT SO LONG AGO WE SAW THINGS IN A TOTALLY DIFFERENT WAY THAN WE DO NOW.**

Because we all recognize that we are in process, along with everyone else, we tend to have grace for one another, especially for those who don't happen to see things the way we currently see them—because not so long ago we saw things in a totally different way than we do now.

This also means that we are less focused on trying to get others to see things our way and more focused on allowing Jesus to transform us into His image.

In other words, we seek a consensus of heart—which is about how we put the words of Jesus into practice—and we're not seeking a consensus of opinion—which is about getting everyone to conform to a set of doctrines and beliefs.

In fact, we actually value the ability to fellowship with those who see things differently. How else can we learn if we only associate with those who already agree with us?

This works beautifully, as long as none of us decides to impose our views on everyone else. As long as we can all hold loosely to our ideas and adopt a posture that says, "I might be wrong", or "I have something to learn from the rest of you", we're in good shape. It's only when someone demands conformity that we're in trouble.

This "Naive Realism" phenomenon exposes our inherent narcissism. We all have a version of reality that places ourselves in the center and elevates our ideas as the standard to which everyone else should conform.

If everyone who drives slower than me is too slow, and if everyone who drives faster is driving too fast, then only those who are doing what I am doing—or thinking like I am thinking—are in the right. This means that only those who are like me are worth listening to and those who aren't like me are inferior.

Does that sound like a way of thinking that Jesus would advocate? Certainly not.

But it does illustrate why Jesus commanded his disciples and followers to do one thing right off the bat: Deny yourself and follow me.

Jesus knows that men and women are selfish at heart. He completely sees how we all live in our own little universe—or kingdom—where we are at the center and everything is oriented to conform to our way of thinking.

Instead, Jesus says that we have to put Him at the center of our lives and we must conform our way of thinking to His. This is what he means when he says, "repent", which means "to think differently."

So, what's our only way out of this trap of self-deception? I think we have to let go of the idea that we are the unbiased standards for excellence. We have to surrender ourselves to Jesus, allowing Him to be our center and our standard. We can't lean on our own understanding. We must orient ourselves towards Jesus and allow Him to guide our thoughts, and actions, and attitudes.

As one friend pointed out to me, Jesus said "Follow me and *I will make you...*", which means transformation is built into the deal.

We have to admit that we need to change, and then we have to confess that we cannot change ourselves apart from Jesus. He makes us into the people we need to be; conformed to His image and filled with His Spirit which is brimming with love, and life and hope and peace that passes understanding.

Put Jesus at the center and then let go of that steering wheel. You'll like where He wants to take you. I promise.

CHAPTER 17

WHEN THE SPIRIT CONTRADICTS THE BIBLE

"Too many, I fear, have made the Bible into an idol and worship it rather than the Holy One it represents. Jesus said He had more truth to reveal than could ever be written. If we are paying attention to the Spirit of Truth, which followed the earthly ministry of Jesus, we will discover truth and wisdom not mentioned in the Bible. If you believe God's truth is limited to the volume written and compiled by men centuries ago, your God is too small."

— CEEJAY GARRETT

Quite often when I suggest that believers today can hear the voice of Jesus and be led by the Holy Spirit, people are quick to say that the Holy Spirit would never contradict anything that had already been written down in the Scriptures.

This knee-jerk reaction is meant to do two things: First, it is meant to maintain the Bible as our ultimate authority. Nothing new or different can ever be introduced into our faith system because God's Word (the Bible) has said everything that will ever need to be said about God.

Secondly, the statement is meant to downplay our experiences and subjugate those experiences to the Scriptures. In effect, all experiences are essentially pointless because anything they might reveal to us, and anything we might learn from those experiences, are subject to correction. Therefore, what good is experience if anything that might be learned from it is already written down in the Book for me?

The problem with this view is that the Scriptures themselves completely contradict this assumption.

Rather than a unified voice of agreement throughout the Bible, what we observe is an ongoing dialog where one prophet says something about God, and then later on another prophet challenges that idea. So, in other words, the Spirit speaks to the prophet who writes down what he hears, and later on another prophet also hears from the Spirit and writes down something that modifies or enhances—or sometimes flatly contradicts—what the previous prophet wrote down.

THIS IS WHAT THE BIBLE IS: A SERIES OF PROGRESSIVELY ENLIGHTENED IDEAS ABOUT WHO GOD IS AND WHAT GOD IS LIKE.

This is what the Bible is: A series of progressively enlightened ideas about who God is and what God is like.

As we've already seen, for example, when Moses says that God requires animal sacrifice and other voices modify this until Jesus gives us the final word on the matter. Or, when Moses introduces the idea of "an eye for an eye and a tooth for a tooth", but Jesus shows up and says, "But I say to you, love your enemies."

Not only this, but Jesus also corrects Moses's statements when He says that God "makes his sun rise on the evil and on the good, and sends rain on the just and on the unjust." (See Matt. 5:45) Because, according to Moses, in Deuteronomy 28:12, God says to the righteous: "The Lord will open to you his good treasury, the heavens, to give the rain to your land in its season and to bless all the work of your hands." But to the unrighteous God says: "The Lord will make the rain of your land powder. From heaven dust shall come down on you until you are destroyed." (v. 24)

Jesus makes it clear in the Sermon on the Mount that Moses was wrong about God's disposition towards people. He loves and blesses them both the same.

Another good example of how some prophetic voices in Scripture correct what has been said previously is when Elijah commands a man named Jehu to strike down the entire house of his master, Ahab. (See 2 Kings 9:7-8) Once he obeys this command, Jehu is praised as a righteous man of God. However, later on the prophet Hosea writes that God spoke to Him saying: *"I will punish the house of Jehu for the blood of Jezreel, and I will put an end to the kingdom of the house of Israel." (Hosea 1:4)*

So, I ask you: Are you still so convinced that the Holy Spirit will never contradict what has been written in the scriptures?

The fact is that the Holy Spirit *almost always* contradicts what has been written in the scriptures. Peter learned that when the voice of the Lord spoke to him and commanded him to kill and eat the unclean animals. The Pharisees learned that when they brought the woman caught in adultery to Jesus. James and John learned that when they asked Jesus if they could call down fire on the Samaritans as Elijah had done. In every single case, if these men had held tightly to their scriptures, they would have missed what Jesus was doing. Peter would not have awakened to God's plan to redeem the Gentiles. The Pharisees would have executed an adulterous woman instead of showing her mercy. James and John would have called down fire upon Samaritans before Philip could come and preach the Good News of the Kingdom to them. (See Acts 8:5)

The surprising truth is: The Holy Spirit will *almost always* contradict what has been written in the scriptures. In fact, we should probably expect it.

Jesus affirms this idea when he rebukes the Pharisees who cannot let go of their Scriptures long enough to accept what they have seen with their eyes and heard with their own ears. They are blinded by their Bibles. The refuse to see that the eyes of the blind were opened and the lame were made whole because it didn't fit with what their Scriptures told them.

So, because what they were seeing didn't line up with what was written, they rejected their experiences of God and attributed the work of the Holy Spirit to Satan. Jesus responded to their blindness and warned them that the unforgivable sin was to reject what the Spirit of God was doing right in front of them.

> "Truly I tell you, people can be forgiven all their sins and every slander they utter, but whoever blasphemes against the Holy Spirit will never be forgiven; they are guilty of an eternal sin." (Mark 3:28-29)

The greatest sin, according to Jesus, is to deny what the Holy Spirit is doing and revealing to you—even if that revelation contradicts what has been written in the Scriptures.

This means that we must be willing to leave the safety and security of our Bibles to walk with Jesus in the uncertain and unknown realm of faith. This is why we are called to "test the spirits" (1 John 4:1) and to use discernment in our walk with Christ. Because we are expected to be venturing out into the deep with Him, not lounging comfortably in our pew clinging tightly to our absolute certainty, but holding fast to Jesus who is untamed and unbound by any book.

Jesus was most critical of the Pharisees because they were mired in the traditions of men (Mark 7:8) and unwilling to accept anything that didn't line up with their understanding of

Scripture. He begged them to see that the life they were seeking for in the Scriptures was only available through Him. They refused to come to Him for life because they were convinced that their Bible had all the answers. (John 5:40)

The Pharisees rejected Jesus because they assumed that the Holy Spirit would never contradict what was written down in their Scriptures. But, they were wrong about that. When the Holy Spirit did something they didn't think aligned with their Book, they attributed that to Satan, and as a result they totally missed the fulfillment of every prophecy in that same Holy Book. He was standing right in front of them, and they missed Him.

Please don't make the same mistake.

"SAD, INDEED, WOULD THE WHOLE MATTER BE, IF THE BIBLE HAD TOLD US EVERYTHING GOD MEANT US TO BELIEVE. BUT HEREIN IS THE BIBLE ITSELF GREATLY WRONGED. IT NOWHERE LAYS CLAIM TO BE REGARDED AS THE WORD, THE WAY, THE TRUTH. THE BIBLE LEADS US TO JESUS, THE INEXHAUSTIBLE, THE EVER UNFOLDING REVELATION OF GOD. IT IS CHRIST 'IN WHOM ARE HID ALL THE TREASURES OF WISDOM AND KNOWLEDGE,' NOT THE BIBLE, SAVE AS LEADING TO HIM."

—GEORGE MACDONALD[1]

CHAPTER 18

RECOVERING THE LOST EPISTLE OF JESUS

"The Word of God is not just written in ink and paper. It's written in flesh and blood. Jesus is the Word. Read the Bible. Follow Jesus."

— NATHAN HAMM

As I have been studying the scriptures and investigating the canon of the New Testament recently, I made a truly remarkable discovery about a lost epistle of Christ.

Now, there are a few epistles of Paul that we know about that have been lost, like the Epistle to the Laodiceans, and an earlier Epistle to the Corinthians that predates our 1 Corinthians, for example. But most Christians, and even many New Testament scholars, do not know that there is one epistle that was delivered by Paul and the Apostles that almost no one has ever read before.

It's true. Paul himself even tells us about this lost epistle in 2 Corinthians and he personally testifies to the fact that it was written by Jesus personally and inspired by the Holy Spirit.

How can this be? How have we missed the existence of an epistle written personally by Jesus and delivered to the early Church by Paul and the other Apostles?

I blame the Pharisees. Not those first-century Jewish teachers of the Law that opposed Jesus, but their spiritual successors who continually search the scriptures for life and miss the actual Author of Life whom the scriptures are pointing to.

There are Pharisees of the New Testament scriptures today, even as there were Pharisees of the Old Testament scriptures then.

> **WE ARE BLIND TO THE LOST EPISTLE OF CHRIST BECAUSE WE CAN'T LOOK PAST THE BIBLE. IT'S LIKE LOOKING AT THE FOREST AND MISSING THE TREE.**

These New Testament Pharisees, and their disciples, hold up the written "Word of God" as having some absolute, unquestionable authority over our lives while ignoring the fact that those same scriptures point to a living "Word of God" who became flesh—not paper—and now lives within each and every one of His children by the power of the Holy Spirit.

Simply put, we are blind to the lost Epistle of Christ because we can't look past the Bible. It's like looking at the forest and missing the tree.

So, what exactly is the "Epistle of Christ" that Paul talks about? Where is it now? What happened to it? Why can't we read it today?

Here's what Paul says about it:

> "You yourselves are our epistle, written on our hearts, to be known and read by all. And you show that you are a letter from Christ delivered by us, written not with ink but with the Spirit of the living God, not on tablets of stone but on tablets of human hearts." (2 Cor. 3:2-3)

The lost Epistle of Christ is you. You are the letter that Jesus wrote, and continues to write, every single day.

As long as you remain in connection with Jesus, He is writing a letter of love on your heart. He writes a new chapter every single day that you are alive, and with every breath you take He writes another verse about His incredible love for you, and His intense desire to change this broken world from the inside out—starting with you.

So, the lost letter of Jesus is written within you, and it is meant to be read by those around you. This means your life should literally be an open book to your family, friends, neighbors, co-workers and acquaintances. The story of Jesus should entice people to read further, to turn the page, and to get lost in those verses of Divine affection.

There is a missing chapter in every Bible ever printed. It's you and your story of Jesus. He intends for it to "be known and read by all."

Don't let this lost letter of Jesus get lost again. Deliver it today.

CHAPTER 19

WHAT IF NO ONE HAD A BIBLE?

"So long as we only see the Logos of God as embodied multifariously in symbols in the letter of Holy Scripture, we have not yet achieved spiritual insight into the incorporeal, simple, single and unique Father as He exists in the incorporeal, simple, single and unique Son... We need such knowledge so that, having first penetrated the veils of the sayings which cover the Logos, we may with a naked intellect see—in so far as men can—the pure Logos, as He exists in Himself, clearly showing us the Father in Himself."

— ST. MAXIMOS, THE CONFESSOR

Try to imagine it: No Bibles anywhere. No King James. No NIV. Not even a paperback copy of *The Message*.

What would that be like?

Regardless of how such a thing might happen, try to imagine what it would be like to never have access to the Bible ever again.

I know this might sound scandalous, but in some ways I think our world might actually be a better place if no one had a Bible anymore.

I wonder if maybe we'd start to discover an inner desperation and a hunger for a deeper experience of Jesus if we didn't depend on a book for everything.

Not only that, if there were no Bibles, we just might start to value listening to one another share testimonies of Jesus. Especially if there was no more need to hear from the resident Bible expert or scholar talk for an hour every weekend.

> IF THERE WERE NO BIBLES, WE JUST MIGHT START TO VALUE LISTENING TO ONE ANOTHER SHARE TESTIMONIES OF JESUS. ESPECIALLY IF THERE WAS NO MORE NEED TO HEAR FROM THE RESIDENT BIBLE EXPERT OR SCHOLAR TALK FOR AN HOUR EVERY WEEKEND.

Imagine sitting around your living room with friends and listening to people share what Jesus was saying or doing in their lives that week. Imagine someone closing their eyes and quoting verses about how nothing can separate us from the love of God, or about how Jesus died for us while we were still enemies of God?

Don't you think this might help us to connect with one another—and with Jesus—more directly?

This is exactly what the early Christian church was like. They did not have copies of Paul's letters in their possession. They did not have a collection of the Hebrew Scriptures in their homes. A scroll of Isaiah, for example, would have been more expensive than most of those poverty-level Christians could ever afford. As noted New Testament scholar Ben Witherington says:

> "A standard roll of papyrus in mid-first century A.D. Egypt cost four drachmae, which is to say it cost about 4-8 days pay (for) an ordinary workman. But let us take for example, the famous Isaiah scroll found at Qumran. A roll thirty feet long took no less than 30 or so hours to fill up. That is—at least three full day's work for a scribe. A copy of Isaiah then could cost at least 10 denarii (or 2 week's pay), and that is a low guess. And then you would have exactly ONE book of the OT in your hands.

Imagine about 40 more rolls that long and you can imagine an
OT on scrolls.¹

So, the average Christian in the first century did not have
access to the scriptures. Yet, somehow, they managed to live radical lives of Christ-like love, sharing all that they had with one
another, and even "turned the world upside down,"(Acts 17:6)
all without owning a Bible.

How did they do that? How did those primitive Christians
know Christ so intimately? How did they face horrific persecu-
tions and survive the worst that the Roman Empire could dish
out without even a copy of the Gospel of John in their back
pocket?

The answer is: They had the Holy Spirit living inside of them.
They had a connection with Jesus, the Risen Lord, that tran-
scended the written word.

Now, to be fair, many of them probably knew a few of the
basic teachings of Jesus passed along to them by other Christians.
There was a very strong oral tradition in the early Christian community and no doubt many of those illiterate believers had a
few of Christ's teachings hidden in their heart. But that's still
part of my point: They had a vibrant, thriving relationship with
the Prince of Peace. He sustained them. He strengthened them.
He walked right beside them every step of the way. It wasn't the
Bible that gave them hope, it was their own personal connection
to Christ.

Maybe I'm the only one, but the more I think about this the
more convinced I am that we might just be better off without
our Bibles today. Maybe without our precious Bibles we might
also cling to Jesus the way those earliest Christians did. Maybe
without our proof-texts and our study guides we might learn
how to rely on the Spirit of God the same way they must have.

Yes, I do realize that we are so blessed to have our Bibles. What I'm talking about is what it would be like to take what we already know the Bible says and moving onward to actually experiencing those words in a deeper way.

I can't help but wonder what it would be like for us to carry the Word of God around in our hearts every day. What if we had to rely on God's indwelling Spirit for every breath and every step? What if we only had our memories of scripture to sustain us?

I also wonder, what scriptures we would choose to pass on to our children if we didn't have a Bible? What verses would we choose to share with them? Perhaps those verses where Jesus says, "Father forgive them, for they know not what they do" and "Love one another as I have loved you" would top your list. Perhaps you'd want your children to remember certain Parables that Jesus shared, like the Prodigal Son, or the Treasure in the Field or the Sower of Seeds.

But, chances are you probably wouldn't find it all that crucial to memorize verses where God commanded His people to slaughter every man, woman and child, or where He warned them not to show any compassion while killing infants. You might want to leave behind the verses about how blessed those people are who dash babies against the rocks.

That, to me, would be a very good thing.

If all we had left was Jesus and our memories of scriptures that really touched us and profoundly changed us, that wouldn't be so bad.

The point of my asking this question is to get us to consider what our faith would be like without depending upon what others wrote 2,000 years ago to share their experiences of Jesus.

Instead, I hope to inspire us to consider that our faith is based on our own experiences of Jesus today.

Let me make it crystal clear: The Bible leads us to Jesus. But what we do with Jesus after that is the most important thing of all.

As we've already seen, some people are convinced that we can never know anything about Jesus or God without the Bible.

But the Bible contradicts that, over and over again.

What the Bible tells us is that we can know Jesus, and the Father, directly, personally and immediately at this very moment. So, if you really believe the Bible, then I would encourage you to do what the Bible says: connect with God yourself. Don't just read about Him—know Him, and listen to Him, and follow Him, and learn to love Him more every day.

Let me assure you of this: if someone took your Bibles away, you would still have Jesus. If every Bible

IF YOUR FAITH WOULD BE HOPELESSLY EMPTY WITHOUT THE BIBLE, THEN YOU MIGHT HAVE A MUCH BIGGER PROBLEM.

on earth was suddenly destroyed, you and I would still hear His voice. If no one ever read the Bible again, God would still be alive and moving and speaking and revealing Himself through His Spirit, and through His people, and through nature, and art, and music, and circumstances.

However, if your faith would be hopelessly empty without the Bible, then you might have a much bigger problem. Maybe you need to ask yourself if you actually have a relationship with God at all? If your faith depends upon a book, then maybe you've only focused on reading and learning information about God, but you've not exactly come to know that same God in any real way yet?

If so, then I most certainly recommend setting your Bible aside. Get to know Jesus. Spend time alone with Him. Talk to Him. Listen to His voice. Practice an awareness of His presence. Reading more Bible verses will not help you encounter Him. In fact, it just might postpone any deeper experiences with Jesus you might have.

You've read about God. You know information about Jesus. That's great. But now it's time to meet Him and to know Him in a deeper way.

Remember: God is not the Bible. The Bible is not God.

Yes, the Bible is a wonderful blessing to us all. We should be very grateful for it. But Jesus transcends and eclipses the Bible in every possible way. He is not bound by a book. He is not constricted into syllables and sentences. He is not captured on a page.

By asking the question: "What if no one had a Bible?" I am inviting you to consider moving on to phase 2 of your life in Christ.

Look up from the page long enough to listen for His still small voice. Close the book long enough to walk with Him today. Maybe even put the Bible back on the shelf just long enough to put what you've read about into practice. You can always come back to it later. It's not going anywhere. But maybe sometimes we need to take off the training wheels and learn to balance ourselves if we really hope to enter the race.

I'll meet you at the top of the hill.

JESUS SUPREME

"In Jesus, God has opened his heart to us. He has turned his face to us. He comes to us, reveals his thoughts, and shows us who he is and what he wills. He gives us everything we need and wants to perfect the work he has begun in us. Amazingly, we feeble and insignificant beings are the object of his concern. Out of the incomprehensible love of his heart, God loves each of us quite personally. In his concern for humankind, God seeks out all people and invites them to take part in his new creation."

— EBERHARD ARNOLD

If you love the Bible, you'll love Jesus even more. He is the Word made flesh. He has come to live among –and within—us.

Nothing—and I mean nothing—can ever separate you from the love of God which is in Christ Jesus. As Paul reminds us:

"Who shall separate us from the love of Christ? Shall tribulation, or distress, or persecution, or famine, or nakedness, or danger, or sword?...No, in all these things we are more than conquerors through him who loved us. For I am sure that neither death nor life, nor angels nor rulers, nor things present nor things to come, nor powers, nor height nor depth, nor anything else in all creation, will be able to separate us from the love of God in Christ Jesus our Lord." (Romans 8:35-39)

He, and the Father, are now alive within you; closer to you than your own heartbeat.

"Jesus answered him, 'If anyone loves me, he will keep my word, and my Father will love him, and we will come to him and make our home with him.'" (John 14:23)

He has promised: *"I will never leave you nor forsake you." (Hebrews 13:5)*

What this means is that you and I will never know what it's like to be apart from Jesus. It means that we will never experience another moment without Jesus. From this very moment, stretching outward into the endless eons of eternity, you and I will remain forever intertwined with Jesus.

> WHAT THIS MEANS IS THAT YOU AND I WILL NEVER KNOW WHAT IT'S LIKE TO BE APART FROM JESUS. IT MEANS THAT WE WILL NEVER EXPERIENCE ANOTHER MOMENT WITHOUT JESUS. FROM THIS VERY MOMENT, STRETCHING OUTWARD INTO THE ENDLESS EONS OF ETERNITY, YOU AND I WILL REMAIN FOREVER INTERTWINED WITH JESUS.

Forever.

Nations will fade. The earth may perish. The universe itself may vanish away. But our connection with Jesus will never end.

Never.

Where there are tongues, they will cease. Where there are religions, they will fail. Where there are books—even Bibles—they will all eventually crumble with age.

But Jesus, who is our life, will never end. He will never fade. He will never cease. Jesus is Love, and His Love endures forever.

My intention and purpose for writing this book was to remind us all that Jesus is our only hope.

The Bible is wonderful, and we should be grateful for the wisdom that it contains. We should be especially grateful for all the many ways it points us to our Lord Jesus. Yes, the Bible is a wonderful book, but it is not Jesus. It does not even come close to how glorious He is.

Remember: Our relationship is not with a book, but with a person. Yes, we may learn more details about this person from the book, but our actual relationship with the Author continues, even after we close that book.

After you close *this* book, my hope is that you will continually develop your hunger to know Jesus more. I pray that you might begin to thirst even more to find yourself in His presence. I encourage you to begin learning how to be still and listen for the voice of the Good Shepherd. I also urge you to seek out and gather with others who are also just as hungry to know Jesus as you are, maybe more so. My own spiritual life has been profoundly changed by an ongoing connection with other brothers and sisters in Christ who want nothing more than to hear His voice, and follow His lead, and put His words into practice together.

I have been following Jesus for over 40 years now and I am convinced of this: knowing things *about* Jesus is wonderful. But I'm here to tell you: knowing Jesus is better than life itself.

I am also convinced that, even though the canon of scripture may have been closed over a thousand years ago, the voices of the Spirit and the Good Shepherd are still speaking today. He has not ever been bound in any book. He will not ever be limited by any language. He shall not be constrained by any copyright.

The truth is: Jesus is closer to you than this book you're reading right now. God has come near. Emmanuel—literally *"God with us"*—is with you always. He has promised to make His home in you. He has vowed to never leave you or forsake you.

For the rest of eternity, you will be in intimate contact with Him. He is closer to you than your own breath. He is more real than your own heartbeat. All you can ever do is know Him more. Your life and His heart are on an unavoidable collision course. This is what you were created for.

His dream is to reveal more of Himself to you today. Whatever you do, please do not miss your opportunity to draw closer to Jesus.

He is waiting for you just outside the boundary of these pages. Do you see Him? Do you hear His voice?

Don't be afraid to draw nearer to Him. He wants to make Himself known to you. That still, small voice? It's Jesus. He is so in love with you. He is so overjoyed at the idea of revealing more of Himself to you, His beloved. He is the Alpha, and the Omega. He is the First and the Last.

He is forever unbound.

ENDNOTES

CHAPTER 3

1. Rohr, Richard, "Daily Meditations," Week 3, Sunday, Jan. 14, 2018

CHAPTER 5

1. As quoted by William Paul Young in this video: https://youtu.be/
   RBSqUsdClYo

2. Ibid.

3. Snyder, Howard, *Christ's Body: The Community of the King*, pp.94-95

CHAPTER 7

1. From Chuck McKnight's blog: http://www.patheos.com/blogs/
   hippieheretic/2017/06/invisible-man-and-his-shadow-allegory.html

2. Torrance, Thomas F., *Divine Meaning: Studies in Patristic Hermeneutics*,
   pp.9-10

CHAPTER 8

1. C.S. Lewis, in a letter dated October 5, 1955

CHAPTER 10

1. Hart, David Bentley, *The New Testament: A Translation*, pg. 336; commentary on 1 Cor. 10:11

CHAPTER 11

1. http://www.patheos.com/blogs/peterenns/2013/07/heres-something-about-the-bible-of-the-first-christians-i-bet-many-of-you-didnt-know-youre-welcome/

CHAPTER 12

1. "Jesus DID Exist", Bart Ehrman, YouTube Video: https://youtu.be/W49XA2IFpYs

2. http://apologetics-notes.comereason.org/2017/09/yes-jesus-existed-even-romans-outside.html

3. Ibid.

4. Dr. Peter Williams, "New Evidences the Gospels Were Based on Eyewitness Accounts", Lanier Theological Library [Video] http://subversive1.blogspot.com/2015/02/are-nt-documents-reliable.html

CHAPTER 14

1. For further reading on this topic, read *What's with Paul and Women?* by Jon Zens

2. Hays, Richard, *The Moral Vision of the New Testament*, pg. 389

CHAPTER 15

1. Ignatius, *Epistle to the Philippians*, v. 8-9

CHAPTER 16

1.   Inspired by an interview with Lee Ross by David McRaney from "You Are Not So Smart" podcast: https://soundcloud.com/youarenotsosmart/062-naive-realism-lee-ross

CHAPTER 17

1.   Unspoken Sermons Series, "The Higher Faith", by George MacDonald

CHAPTER 19

1.   From Ben Witheringtons' blog: http://www.patheos.com/blogs/bibleandculture/2011/11/05/books-and-scrolls-in-the-world-of-jesus/

For more information about Keith Giles
or to contact him for speaking engagements,
please visit *www.KeithGiles.com*

Many voices. One message.

Quoir is a boutique publishing company
with a single message: Christ is all.
Our books explore both His
cosmic nature and corporate expression.

For more information, please visit
www.quoir.com

CPSIA information can be obtained
at www.ICGtesting.com
Printed in the USA
BVHW080839081019
560521BV00015B/265/P